SPRING 62

A JOURNAL OF

ARCHETYPE

AND

CULTURE

Fall and Winter, 1997

SPRING JOURNAL

WOODSTOCK, CONNECTICUT 06281

ACKNOWLEDGMENTS

To Princeton University Press for quotations from the *Collected Works (CW)* of C. G. Jung (Bollingen Series XX), translated by R. F. C. Hull, edited by H. Read, M. Fordham, G. Adler, and Wm. McGuire, and published in Great Britain by Routledge and Kegan Paul, London. Other quotations have been acknowledged throughout in appropriate notes and references.

Spring is printed in the United States of America, text on acid free paper.

Spring is the oldest Jungian journal in the world. It was founded in 1941 by the Analytical Psychology Club of New York. In 1970, James Hillman transferred its editing and publication to Zürich, Switzerland. From 1978 to 1988, it was edited in Dallas, Texas. Since 1988 it has been edited in Connecticut.

CONTENTS

SPRING 62: AMERICAN SOUL

In 1941, the Analytical Psychology Club of New York started publication of an annual journal called *Spring*. It was for the most part edited and subsidized by Jane Pratt, who would leave her farm in Bridgewater, Connecticut once a week to go to the city for editorial meetings with her board. In 1969, still in charge yet getting on in years (and according to her daughter, still "locking herself away" every week until she had got every article perfect), Jane decided that *Spring* needed some "new blood." She proposed to James Hillman, at that time a practicing analytical psychologist and the former director of studies at the Jung Institute in Zürich, that he take over.

Hillman accepted Pratt's offer and took over the editorship of the journal expanding its reach to the publication of books as well. For the next three decades, beginning in Zürich, then from Dallas and Connecticut, he has seen to it that every "i" was dotted and every "t" was crossed in literally every manuscript published. Writers who submitted papers over those years were often surprised, and sometimes consternated, to get them back with every sentence washed clean of all but the most essential points. If there was one word that especially appeared in his criticisms it was "cut." "Shorten" was a close second. These were not at all words that, to put it mildly, most writers were accustomed to.

With this issue, alas, James is announcing his retirement from the senior editorship of the journal. (He will continue to preside over Spring Publications.) At age seventy-two, having become a best-selling author and one of the world's busiest lecturers, he can hardly be blamed for wanting to give up the drudgery of the editor's pencil. We will miss his guiding hand but promise to keep the pencil as sharp as ever, even if the elegance with which he wielded it is irreplaceable.

"American Soul," appropriately, is about as Hillmanic a subject as you can get. Soul is a word that entered the American vocabulary in a new way around 1975, thanks largely to the influence of Hillman's groundbreaking book, *Re-visioning Psychology* (and before that in *Suicide and the Soul*). After *Re-visioning*, soul was no longer to be merely the property of a religious doctrine, or of jazz and black culture, or a certain kind of food, but a special kind of psychological identity as well, with Saturnian and Hermetic roots in the Italian Renaissance.

Since there are still some cynical types out there who think "American Soul" is the perfect oxymoron, we offer in this issue at least a start in confusing them. From Christopher Columbus himself (speaking of the Italian Renaissance) to the stress syndromes of the Vietnam War, from the archetypal sinking of the Titanic to a dinner with Anaïs Nin, this issue "re-visions" many manisfestations of soul in American life. We are particularly honored that Gary Hart, the distinguished former United States Senator from Colorado and Oxford Fellow, contributes a piece to the discussion.

In one guise or another, of course, since its founding in the darkest days of World War II, *Spring* has been bringing you American Soul all along. "Soul-making," as Hillman calls it, is anywhere you can see or find it. *Spring's* ongoing task, as always, is to keep trying to see or find it in exactly the places you might least expect.

— The Editors

Toward a New American Myth

GARY HART

A rmed with the thunderbolt given him by the Cyclops and
having liberated his brother gods and sister goddesses from
their devourer Cronus, the greatest of the ancient Greek
gods, Zeus, defeated the Titans under Atlas with the aid of the
Hundred-handed Ones. Zeus himself, to commemorate his victory,
set up at Delphi the stone disgorged by Cronus—who had swallowed it
mistakenly thinking it to be the infant Zeus.

And thus began ancient Hellenic myth and the Greek culture
which was to become the very foundation of Western civilization.
Except for its decline during the recent age of Enlightenment, myth
has continued to be the basis for ours and other civilizations for
more than four thousand years.

I want to propose the creation of a *new* American myth for the
twenty first century and the new millennium. For the American
nation requires a new myth—a myth that defines its national
purpose, animates its values and directs its course for the next
century. But our new self-defining myth will resonate *only* if it
accounts for the turbulent social revolutions of the late twentieth
century, *only* if it destroys old stereotypes and guides the behavior

Gary Hart is an international lawyer, former United States Senator, author of nine
books, and visiting fellow at Oxford University (1996).

of genders, races and cultures toward each other, and *only* if it re-creates a bond between humanity and nature. The derivation of this new national myth must engage our most creative energies and fertile imaginations if we are to tell America's story in the next millennium.

Every nation, every people, consciously or unconsciously require a myth—a narrative of identity and ideal flowing from the collective unconscious that accounts for society's victories and defeats. Thus we have "Mother Russia," Germany's Teutonic Knight, China's Middle Kingdom, France's Joan of Arc.

Myths both derive from and create the cultures they enliven. And myths magically evolve to account for changing times. In our three-hundred year existence as a people we have shared many myths: the myth of pilgrim; the myth of colonial; the myth of revolutionary; the myth of frontiersman, pioneer and explorer; the great myth of cowboy—so vital even today; the myth of settler and broadshouldered city builder; the myth of railroad builder and steelmaker; the myth of doughboy—democracy's defender against imperialism, fascism and communism; and, most recently, the myth of space explorer. In each case the center of the myth is always a personalized, idealized icon embodying the qualities history, memory and imagination have led us to *believe* we represent.

These myths concern both who we are and who we *tell* ourselves we are. They generate our novels, our poems, our films, our music and our imaginations. We create these myths and they in turn create *us*. Our myths are as "real" as our imaginations can make them. What is the film *Pocahontas* but a modern animated version of a nature myth based upon a more-or-less true story of relations between native Americans and early pilgrims? What are William Faulkner's novels but the cultural and racial revolutions of the post-Civil War South compressed into the mythically-real County of Yoknapatawpha? What is *The Old Man and the Sea* but Hemingway's epic myth of an old but indomitable hero's struggle with a force of nature as palpable, yet as mythical, as Faulkner's immobile and dimensionless bear and Melville's great white whale? What is John Wayne, whose name is given to airports and whose face adorns pathetic souvenir plates, but the tangible modern re-creation of ten thousand mythical cowboys who were clear-eyed, courageous and straight-shooting beyond human capacity or realistic belief? And what of John Kennedy who compressed charisma and tragedy into such a brief shining moment as to guarantee immortality in the pantheon of political heroes of the ages? What is the Star Wars saga but Luke Skywalker's classic heroic quest into the underworld of space for the grail of knowledge required to liberate his people?

Each of us can think of dozens of such mythological examples in both high and popular cultures, in movies, in books, in politics and music. Humble but triumphant Rockys; superhuman Rambos and Terminators; immortal Elvises and Marilyns; the martyred dreamer of trans-racial justice Martin Luther King, Jr.; in all cases the myth encompasses what the character, real or imagined, was *and* what we wanted him or her to be. Yet even as we surround ourselves—perhaps insulate ourselves—with mundane myths from the popular culture, we seem to lack the great defining myths that create aspiration and make great deeds possible. We do so because our heroes have let us down, some by permitting themselves to be assassinated, and because—even as we seek to immortalize the Elvises and Marilyns—we really don't *believe* in myth.

The very word "myth" is today synonymous with fairytale, fantasy, chimera or outright falsehood. To call something a "myth" is a strong form of dismissal and rejection. To be "mythical" is to have entered the twentieth century's most shameful realm, the realm of that which cannot be empirically, logically, analytically or scientifically verified. For we are the late great-great grandchildren of the Enlightenment, that monumental eighteenth century liberation of the human mind from suspicion and fear so that it could question, dissect, analyze and reduce. Power perceptibly removed itself during the Enlightenment from the mysteries of the ecclesiastical confessional to the empirically certifiable scientific laboratory. And as the Enlightenment enthroned reason, reason enthroned science, science enthroned technology, twentieth century technology enthroned modernity, modernity enthroned materialism, and materialism, as the century closed, begat consumption.

Consumption, by definition, is insatiable. Once it has consumed four television sets, three walkmen, two computers, a closetful of Levis, an orgiastic revelry of Big Macs with cheese and Haagen-Daz shakes, it looks around for something else to consume. So it consumes time—with sitcoms; it consumes energy—with televised sports; it consumes creativity and imagination—with sub-mythical fantasies that require neither thought nor spiritual belief. The age of consumption has consumed all our old myths—as evidenced by the same movie plots being recycled with Roman numerals. It has consumed the energy, time and imagination of future mythmakers. And it is even consuming our political leaders before they have the chance to become icons or heroes.

"Technology," according to one scholar, "is the knack of so arranging the world that we do not experience it." Myths require wonder, dread of the unknown, curiosity about first causes, mystical belief, creative imagination and, most of all, the unquenchable desire to tell stories and hear stories told. Consider why most children are born with these qualities and why virtually none of them survive to maturity with any of these qualities intact. The age of consumption devours myths and the wonder necessary to keep myths alive.

It did not require the Greeks huddling under a shower of thunderbolts and lightning flashes four thousand years ago at the foot of Mount Olympus 170 million U.S. Dollars—the cost of a new Hollywood movie—to create a story about a god named Zeus who ruled all the other gods and who was at this moment very angry with someone. Who is he angry at, and why? they asked themselves. And thus a myth was born. As our current film and fiction stories become more expensive and sensational, they also become less engaging, less memorable, and less satisfying. For they cannot re-create the ground of myth, namely that which answers our questions about the structure of the universe, about the relationship of human to nature, and most of all about rules for governing man's behavior toward his brothers and sisters.

In his recent great book *Landscape and Memory*, the historian Simon Schama says this: "...if the entire history of landscape in the West is indeed just a mindless race toward a machine-driven universe, uncomplicated by myth, metaphor and allegory, where measurement, not memory, is the absolute arbiter of value, where our ingenuity is our tragedy, then we are indeed trapped in the engine of our self-destruction." But he continues by offering a rescue path: "What we need," he says, "are new 'creation myths' to repair the damage done by our recklessly mechanical abuse of nature and to restore the balance between man and the rest of the organisms with which he shares the planet."

Be practical, you say. (This insistence on practicality being yet another manifestation of the age of science and logic.) What good can myth do in solving modern problems like health-care cost containment? We don't need a myth for this—we need a *program*. But programs manifestly come from what we call policies. And policies come from social values. And values come from a system of beliefs. And our beliefs come from religious faith. And our religious faiths are profoundly rooted, in the very best sense of the word, in myth. Not myths dismissable as mad fairytales. But myths that give spiritual context to a chaotic universe, myths that create prototypes for human behavior, myths that help us understand irrational death in Oklahoma City and perverse slaughter in Bosnia, myths that underwrite our common purpose and elevate our imaginations so that we can break down old stereotypes, old institutions, old political arrangements and find the courage to pay for a health care system demanded of a *civilized* society. For, as Joseph Campbell has written, "It has always been on myths that the moral orders of societies have been founded."

America today suffers greatly from the disappearance of an energizing myth, a spiritual force sufficiently compelling to propel us into the next millennium. If the Democratic myth in the mid-twentieth century was that a benign national government could create and maintain an affordable social safety net for the middle class and the poor, then the Republican myth now replacing it is that the rising tide of free enterprise capitalism will lift all boats. Take your pick. Both are based upon mythical belief, one in the effectiveness of government and the other in the magic of the market place. But neither truly offers a compelling vision of a greater future, a future beyond consumption, a future where the genders and races unite, a future where humanity respects nature.

Where are our mythmakers, our storytellers, our visionaries? Sitting, I am afraid, in front of a television set, eating junk food, and cursing our nation's government. Where are our new heroes and leaders? Largely contemplating their broker's statement and disdainfully rejecting the ritual, often savage hazing required to join the dubious fraternity of political leadership. Meanwhile, our most creative minds are turning out, and we are paying to watch, humorless, gimmick-ridden, fantastically boring films and videos. We are, in Professor Neil Postman's rightly-famous phrase, "amusing ourselves to death."

But there *is* hope for a new myth, a hope grounded in the possibility that the age of science-bred consumption may be running its course, a hope that the human spirit may be demanding a larger vision than that provided by yet another generation of technical toys designed for personal amusement or military destructiveness. The ancient and resilient Arthurian legend comes to life yet again in the film, *First Knight* and Deepak Chopra's new novel, *The Return of Merlin*. Films like *The Secret of Roan Inish* re-create antique Celtic legends relating to humanity and nature. Increasing numbers of books and films are resorting to the endlessly rich storehouse of native American myth drawn from the complex, pantheistic spiritual world whose values we have tragically neglected or never learned. "New Age" books, music, and retreats offer at least a superficial approach to mythical appreciation. The televised Joseph Campbell series generated a surprisingly large and responsive audience. Large numbers of people, left spiritually unsatisfied by an age of materialism and consumption and unfulfilled by the mechanisms of science, now seek an honorable legend to provide personal, social, cultural and national purpose.

Most immediate and moving perhaps is the vivid testimony of those rare few on the cusp of technology and myth, the space explorers of America and Russia. To a person their conclusions are the same—from the vast ocean of space this terrestrial globe, this earth, looks incredibly blue, green and white and it looks small enough that all those on it should be able to live together. What Homer, Euripides, or Hesiod might have made of such a thought! And what a starting point for a new myth to live by.

As an experiment, and taking our cue from a recent popular movie, let's call our new mythology *Legends of Redemption*. Robert Graves wrote: "A large part of Greek myth is politico-religious history." In American—as in other nations'—mythology, that which is deplorable, such as slavery and injustice, must be included with that which is noble in that history. Edith Hamilton, the classical mythologist, wrote that, with the rise of Greece, "mankind became the center of the universe, the most important thing in it. The Greeks made the gods in their own image." But she also noted that, "the real interest of the myths is that they lead us back to a time when the world was young and the people had a connection with the earth..." A new American myth must restore the people's connection with the earth, a connection so important to those we dispossessed here. The psychologist Rollo May claimed that we lack modern myths because we have confused celebrity with heroism. A new American myth must replace the symbols of celebrity with genuine heroes and symbols of courage, humanity and nobility.

What then are the filaments of a new myth of redemption? Perhaps we have seen the dawn of such redemption in the recent declaration by the Southern Baptist Church extending to all African-Americans, the heirs of generations of slavery, regrets and apologies for its contribution to those institutions that enslaved them. It was for the Southern Baptists an historic, virtually unprecedented act of repentance and social redemption. Is it too much to hope that other institutions in our civil society which participated, in equal or greater measure, in the evils of racism might find similar courage to repent and seek reconciliation? If so, then it might also be hoped that male-dominated institutions, consciously or unconsciously responsible for discrimination against women, could seek full reconciliation of the genders.

There would be mythical symmetry, as well as human justice, in this. Robert Graves suggests that second-millennium B.C. Hellenic invasions of the area now known as Greece caused clashes between, then mergers of, military aristocracies featuring patrilineal succession and pre-Hellenic female theocracies based upon matriarchal traditions. In other words, the earliest myths sprang from mother-goddess worshipping societies which were gradually replaced by male-dominated, military-based societies featuring patrilineal succession; and many of the most enduring Greek myths relate the reconciliation of these two powerful traditions. Thus, the classic Olympian mythic system featured a divine family of six gods and six goddesses. Significantly enough, however, Graves writes, "Patrilineal descent, succession, and inheritance," that is, male-dominated societies, "discourage further myth-making." Could it be that reconciliation based upon full equality between the genders might restore the Olympian ideal of balance between gods and goddesses and redeem the promise of mythic justice?

As complex as reconciliation between genders and among races may prove, even more complex may be the reconciliation between man and nature. This is so in large part because our present consumption-based economy has become tragically dependent upon environmental degradation. Even more, additional nations in Asia, Africa and Latin America, seeking to achieve just a fraction of American life-styles, are emulating the very worst of our industrial excesses in a desperate effort to catch up. Yet, four thousand years after the early Greeks used myth to relate their companionship with nature, perhaps a new American mythology can begin with humanity's redemption of nature and restoration of its connection with the earth. What better way to do so than to redeem our relationship with the first Americans and seek their intercession on our behalf with Mother Earth.

My premise here is simple: the singular opportunity to create a new American myth presented by the advent of a new century and new millennium, and by the end of the Cold War and the close of the industrial age, can be realized only if the white and male American communities are now willing to redeem their birthrights through full reconciliation with the heirs of slavery and the native Americans, as well as with their sister Americans, and only if all Americans restore respect for the earth. Until these commitments are carried out, until we have the courage to clear the moral ledger, then America will continue to drift—without direction, without purpose, and without a dream.

Once redemption is sought in human and natural relationships, however, the new American myth might begin this way:

> From the celestial firmament, the greatest of the gods, Love, who takes alternative male and female forms, and who both bred and birthed the other gods and goddesses, called a Council of Gods and invited them to consider their special playground, the planet earth. "See how beautiful and small it is," Love said, "and yet its favored people, the Americans, fail to achieve their great promise because they still insist on foolishly judging each other by color and gender and persist in defiling the earth. I say let's give them one more chance—say one more generation—to reconcile their petty differences, and if they refuse, we'll judge them harshly and choose another favored people..."

Thus begins the Myth of America's Redemption. It is for young America to complete the myth and to redeem the promise.

CULTURE AND THE ANIMAL SOUL

JAMES HILLMAN

I. An Invocation

B efore we begin, before we utter a word about our human situation, its soul's dilemmas and prospects, we must recall that we raise these questions in a terrain of animals, the aboriginal inhabitants of this earth, this air, these waters—that we are their guests, even if continually their conquerors and executioners, sometimes their protectors. May our recollection of this fact that we are their uneasy guests, especially of their smallest members, the parasites, mites, ants, spiders, and beetles, offer a tribute to their never-failing presence. May they not be offended by anything we say here.

An invocation is not only a literal appeal to invisible spirits, not only a remembrance, an offering, a propitiation; as well, it displaces the human subject from center stage to the wings (*flanco*), an appropriate un-modernist gesture that neglects the ego, the hero, the intentions and biography of the person, of all persons, instead drawing attention sideways, the sideways look, not back to a primitive terror or forward to a future of solutions, but sideways to the soul's habitation extended in the world, elsewhere, and unbounded by the human skin, human concerns and human predictions.

James Hillman is the retiring Senior Editor of this journal and is the publisher of Spring Books.

Further, the invocation to the beast drops the question of geography from the stale thematics of conflicting continents, of conflicting languages, of conflicting Christianisms—those tiresome dilemmas of North and South, of English and Spanish, of Catholic and Protestant, of tribal and urban, drops our geographical reflection to the non-historical, cyclical, organic geography of the animal soul where patriotism has no place and money makes no sense at all. *Fixate*! To escape from economics!

II. A Disclaimer

After the invocation comes the disclaimer—that you, my hosts, for all your generosity in invitation, your efficiency in organization and intelligence in vision have, by inviting me to open this convocation and to focus its themes, yes, you have made a grand error! For I am born in New Jersey on the Atlantic Ocean and emerged from my mother's womb facing over the sea toward Europe, and then educated in a language style that enjoys short sentences, a style whose realism is without magic, devoid of flourish, strict in vocabulary and with a careful Puritan ban on the erotics of adjectives and the qualifying impediments to action of adverbs, a style whose notion of a "good idea" is one that can fix a stalled motor, invent a new tool, or make a quick buck.

Besides, psychology, the profession which claims me, lives in a land of conceptual realism where the native animal magnetism of the soul has been encapsulated by such terms as transference, suggestion, borderline, and synchronicity. A profession that deliberately retreats from John Keats's admonition against "the irritable reaching for reason and fact" because it condemns as pathological the soul's land of "negative capability."

And so, because of psychology, those constituents of actual life lived on earth that are the very stuff of both psychology and poetics—I mean Family, Sexuality, Death, Loyalty, Injustice, Absurdity, Obsession, the Animism of things and places, details of the senses, the irreality of History and the reality of Tragedy—these vital constituents of life on earth have, owing to psychology, been rationalized and literalized into "problems." So if there is one thing we shall avoid in these days together, one Devil we shall ask to be banned from the room, it shall be the Problem. *No hay problema.*

The Devil has a host of little devils in his train, much as the Gods of Neoplatonism could be distinguished by the sorts of archons, principles, daimons and minor personalities who followed and preceded each God. So, too, the "problem" is preceded by small worries and larger obsessions whose main function is to elevate "the Problem" into the highest rank of importance, all the while disguising the fatal feel of the tragic (as if tragedy were a Problem) and also the composting decay of civilization as it releases eruptions of culture and nourishes soul-making by means of fermentations and putrefactions.

So, to repeat the disclaimer, though you have invited a psychologist, we shall not be indulging in the therapy of anxieties, guilts, worries and problems. Worry itself is a demon who has been converted by psychology from a useful animal function to one wholly internal. "I worry," alone, inside myself. Once, however, "worry" referred to a direct action, as a dog worries a bone, a captain worries the enemy by laying siege to a fortress. But now worry is subjective, all internal. I waken at night and worry myself—my future, my marriage, my children—rather than actually worrying, attacking, laying siege to the future, the children, the marriage with reflexive actions. This little example intends merely to free us from our psychological predicament: We are unable to envision the soul's life and the soul's world apart from psychology. And so this disclaimer is also my way of renouncing psychology as the mode of entry to our themes.

III. Three Excursions on History

Oppression and History: There are no problems until we imagine solutions. Problems begin in their solutions. When we wish something, anything, to go away, then it stands as an obstacle, very hard, very literal indeed. Precisely, this hardness is implied by the original meaning of the word "problem." It arrives in our mouths via unyielding military redoubts, via mathematics and chess and logic. A problem, according to the dictionary, is something thrown up at us asking for a solution, such as a riddle or an enigma.

Abandon the idea of solutions, and problems cannot exist. Instead there is an enigma, from the Greek *ainigma*, meaning all things with a second sense, symbols, oracles, mysteries, secrets.

So, let us say each problem contains a secret, is the emblem of a secret or, better said, is a secret emblem, secretly an emblem, and it is for the reason of this secret that we carry problems with us, treasure them, idolize them, carry them as our banners—I have a health problem, a mother problem, a drug problem, a money problem. Under these emblems we march forward into our day.

Civilization, too, marches forward by "solving" its problems, as the Roman engineers invented their bricks and arches to build their bridges and aqueducts to solve the problem of unifying their wide empire. And even as we speak, especially in this city, civilization marches forward by focusing on one big problem, the world economic problem—the homeless and the hungry, the unjust distribution of land and goods, the disruption of balance and the destruction of nature—in short, the weight of economic oppression and the imagination of consumption as liberation.

What is this mystery of oppression and liberation now captured by the problem of economics? Here for a moment I must remind you that economics has taken prisoner many secrets of the soul so that we forget they once were expressions of moral beauty and human collaboration: trust, credit, guarantee, obligation, bond, share, security, saving, interest, balance, warrant, deed, loss, foundation. So, too, oppression is not merely an economic problem; it needs as well to be considered a mysterious emblem, whether conceived in Feminist terms, in Freudian terms, in Marxist terms, always the riddle of *los de abajo*, the peasant, the proletariat, the indigenous peoples, the enslaved, the women, the children, the illiterate, the young, the aged, the darker-skinned, the urban dislocated, the physically impaired and handicapped, the exiles, migrants, imprisoned—always the oppressed.

And this unsolvable oppression gives rise to that other popular problem and its programs: the call for freedom, human rights, equality, choice, opportunity. The idea of freedom arises from the mystery of oppression. History never lets us forget oppression, in fact, history records itself in the documents of oppression, from the earliest conquests of the New World, through slave trade and financial exploitations and missionary conversion—oppressions by guns, by diseases, by alcohol, by laws and crucifixes.

Oppression as a problem of history, even, history as oppression itself; yes, but what of oppression as an emblem of culture?

Our question begins to turn. Instead of the question: "What is the problem of the New World—why does it originate in and maintain itself by oppression?"—instead let us ask: "What is the secret of the New World, of what is this hemisphere emblematic so that its soul feels oppressed, and must imagine experiments in freedom, revolution for freedom, Great Liberators and Declarations of Independence, Bills of Rights and Four Freedoms? What is this yoke in the cosmic imagination? What secret sits in oppression, like an archetypal Grand Inquisitor wearing different dress in different centuries: imperialist, colonial, *blanco*, yanqui, banker, patriarchy, Church, prelate, financial boss, United Fruit Co., Rockefeller, Trade Agreement, drug lord, colonel, F16, George Bush . . . ?

If oppression is archetypal, as the ubiquitous, repetitious and relentless affliction of Hemisphere, an oppression which oscillates between indolent fatalism and frenetic consumption, then its secret is beyond personal psychologies and historical determinants. Neither manic-depressive personality disorders nor histories of repression and revolution can reach the deeper ground that lies in the geographical soil of an entire hemisphere, the animal soul shared by two continents.

To grasp oppression more fully we must step down and behind the human altogether and pose our question to the animal soul. What in the cosmic imagination allows the animal soul, in so many moral and intellectual systems of thought, to be ranked below? What is this willingness on the part of the animal to enter domestication, to be bred, hunted and trapped, to be subject to experimentation, to be beast of burden, to yield its aesthetic displays—skins and horns, feathers and shells—to be so tastily and nourishingly edible and—above all—to partake with its sacrificial slaughter in rituals that serve the Gods? This "oppression" has been portrayed, is being portrayed, as the result of human perversity; but what in the animal's own nature makes this possibility? What is the cosmic significance of what we understand only as oppression? For some peoples, animals are not, never can be, oppressed since they are divinities; in fact, for some peoples, the animals gave us both fire and speech. How so? Because the rich give to the poor, and in the beginning they had it all, and humans had nothing, so they gave us those gifts we now assume to be only human possessions. Always, everywhere, they have been the teachers.

What is there to learn here? Is the oppression of the animal soul a lesson in metamorphosis and re-incarnation? A lesson in the supreme justice of natural law, that all beings have their pre-ordained place? Or, is it a lesson in evolution that the animal soul is fundamentally oppressed because it is lower in the great chain of progressive being in which human intellectual reason is, of course, at the top? Or could the oppression of the animal be teaching us something else?

We do not speak of plants and trees as oppressed, though we hack the underbrush, mow the grass and chainsaw the timber; we don't imagine rocks and soil oppressed though we mine, crush and smelt the former, and tread and harrow the latter. Only the animal kingdom, as it says in the Bible, shall suffer the human heel, and all creatures on earth are here as human helpers. In fact, these creatures do not even know their own names.

The current despair of animals in the face of their extinction is today met with human nostalgia for freedom in a primitive Eden. But freedom is only a sentimentally contemporary reading; service is their actuality. For, in the essence of the animal soul there must lie a willingness, a docility, an innate knowledge of service, now called ecological interdependence, a knowledge that all existence is predicated upon the very lack of freedom, within that inescapable enclosure not only of the great food chain, but within the yoke of mortality to the immortals.

An Inuit (Eskimo) said to Rasmussen that the great sadness of life is that we are always eating what is alive. His statement reflects something archetypal beyond the ecological idea of the great food chain which reduces to a paranoid anxiety of predation and material necessity the cosmic chains of service, and its tragic sadness, called Moira by the Greeks, who oppresses even the Gods within limits. The eternal laws governing the animal imagination and which the actual animal serves led Jung to write that animals are utterly law-abiding, beyond good and evil, unable to stray from the path because they do not have the hubris, the willfulness of the human ego, the possibility of affronting Moira.

This Hemisphere can envision the feelings of oppression permeating the New World, and the acts of oppression and rebellions against oppression, from an additional vantage point than those found in Marxist history books and Feminist sociology texts. Maybe that is why this Hemisphere cannot escape these feelings. It is bound by the cosmic imagination to find out something different and fresh about oppression, for which it can locate its reflection in the overwhelming immensity of this Hemisphere's animal nature, the Americas as a living animal body—the teeming vibration of insects, quivering fish in jungle rivers, flocks of parrots, black caves of a million bats, Chilean rocks covered with sea birds, pink clouds of flamingos in Florida, miles of buffalo in Nebraska and Wyoming, of caribou on Canada's tundra.

Animals prove that to be oppressed is not to be vanquished. In fact, we turn to animal life for evidence of survival through eons, just as animals for most indigenous peoples are the guarantors of survival. The yoke of oppression does not have to be thrown off literally to lift oppression. Oppression can be "lifted" by revision, that is, by placing oppression itself in service to a wider imagination of inhuman archetypal powers. They provide deeper significance to all occasions of existence. Sometimes, in the eyes, or through the eyes, of animals, we can see the tragic sadness and beauty of ineluctable service to these powers that are not human.

There is a second secret in our hemispheric dedication to oppression. This is the mythologem that invented the "New" World. What fantasy, what cosmic imagination held the minds of the intrepid European adventurers? This we all know from schoolbooks: like Prophets, their minds were filled with visions and dreams. The Fountain of Youth, The Seven Cities of Coronado, The Circumnavigation of the Globe, Lost Atlantis, *Tierra del Fuego*,

The Impossible Connection either as Northwest Passage or double flowing river between the Orinoco and the Amazon. The Lost Tribe of Israel, the Tribe of Amazon Women, the most precious grail and garden as Florida, Virginia, Corpus Christi, Vera Cruz. The most precious jewels and metals: Argentina, Rio del Plata, Esmeralda, Columbia—and all things New: New Spain, New England, Newfoundland, New York, New Leon, even New Jersey; and the spices that the three Kings brought to the Infant Lord; and finally, above all, El Dorado, the crazed appetite for Gold.

The imagination that invented the New World together with the secret oppression in its heart is quite clearly the same imagination of alchemy, which, within enclosed introverted laboratories and hermetically sealed language, sought above all else, Gold. Its fantasy worked with silver and jewels, imagined rare birds of all colors and prized the dove, configured strange unknown Kings and Queens, attempted the impossible in the perfection of the rotundum, in the rebirth of age into youth via the alchemical fountain, all driven by the redemptive image of Gold.

The project of the new world is an alchemical projection of renewal, an extraversion of European alchemy's introversion. The New World carries in its psychic substrate an alchemical desire for redemption by transformation of material nature. The New World, from its beginning as a "new" world, is thus a geographical alchemical retort, a labyrinthine laboratory, continually experimenting, continually laboring to transform the leaden weight, the *massa confusa* and *materia prima* of physis into the gold of noble and sophisticated accomplishments. Mining the raw and processing it into the cooked—Bolivian tin, Brazilian timber, Chilean copper, the huge deposits of bauxite, iron, emeralds, oil, coal, nickel—this became the opus of the Americas.

With this extraversion of alchemy into a geographical project an inevitable concretization occurred. Classic alchemy warned ever and again: "Beware of the physical in the material." The Gold of alchemy was not the usual gold that is smelted, not metallic gold, monetary gold, but a noble and sophisticated elixir, a condition of soul. But with the extraversion into the Americas, this gold petrified, became that mineral madness obsessing the conquistadores into modern times, and appropriately named "black" gold of the Maricaibo oil wells, a "gold" still being sought in the wilds of Ecuador and the depths of the Mexican Gulf.

The sense of oppression in the New World—that it is born vanquished, conquered, exploited, that it must throw off the yoke—testifies to a loss. Escaped from its vessel of interiority the soul arrives in the New World stripped, in exile, a migrant victim clutching at anything "new," imagining a new containment in geography. In this state of extreme vulnerability, exposed to an elemental nature and denying its exhausted sensitivity with a sulfuric fury of action, the migrant soul expects the New World to offer gold in the rivers and streets of extraversion.

And what does it meet? *Les tristes tropiques*, the plains without horizon, the swamps and pampas, the placid indifferent rivers, ropes and sheets of endless rains, the melancholy torpor of equatorial heat, and that green tangled darkness of devouring forests so very, very green, the precise color of Hope, yet concealing the primeval serpent, disease and death; green hope ironically betrayed into a place of no hope, hope abandoned which, when translated by the mythic imagination of the European, becomes the soul's abandonment in Hell, no exit.

Even more oppressive than this deceitful emerald city of America's nature is the plain fact of the indigenous peoples who can be at home in "Hell," who live wholly inside this new world without any conception of it as "new." These natives at once became symbolic representatives not only of Hell's denizens and the denial of Christ, but the denial of civilization, of money, of history, and of the very fantasy of renewal that spurred the European effort to "discover" them in the first place. Of course they must be ignored, converted or killed—as residents of Hell, were they not already soulless and dead?

If the secret within the "oppression problem" that we are tracking here leads to the Hell given with the alchemical fantasy of a "new" world, then only by seeing through this idea of the "new" can the American spirit make a fundamental move. The exit from Hell is to abandon the hope that makes the Hell, America's dominant myth, Newness.

"Newness" excites the American mind with the delirium of development. Development—not magic, or virtue, or beauty, or *charis*—governs our endeavors: developing land, developing economies, products, technologies, our personalities. We value even the arts in terms of new developments. We seem to be always progressing from the old to the new, always recapitulating the ocean-crossing, heroically each of us a captain of our fates, a pioneer, conquistador, converting whatever is unknown, strange, spontaneous or odd into the single category of newness, with our backs always turned against the old, Old Castille, Old King George—all the while secretly oppressed, not by the old, but by the designation of this Hemisphere as "New," forcing Americans to a manifest destiny of development, ever wider wings on the Puer who discards what is for what might be, ever more virginities to penetrate and own. The aging-terrified, limelight craving, throwaway civilization begins in the fantasy of this, a "New" World.

But the geography is not new, only history declares it so. The plateaus are of the most ancient geology, the anacondas and abalones, the condors and caimans are not new, nor were the Caribes that lined the shores and danced on the islands. The most clever of all oppressions carried over the seas to this Hemisphere is the fantasy of a "new" World. Newness still remains the Americas' prison.

History and Geography: Rather than "The History of Oppression in the Americas" we are investigating "The Oppression of History in the Americas." For history invaded and captured Americas' geographies. European history—its incests and sibling rivalries, its religious wars, its competitions—Phillip and Elizabeth—its crusading mission to "civilize" all its pomposities, delusions and greeds, carried over in little ships, converted the complex varieties of geographical peoples into a unified historical fantasy of "Indians." Not only that conversion, but the conversion of its geography into "heathen and barbarous landes" since they were not "actually possessed by any Christian Prynce or inhabited by Christian people." So it was written in Walter Raleigh's patent in 1584 prior to his obscure trips to Guyana and the Orinoco.

History in conflict with geography, or shall we say Time in conflict with Place. This, too, is archetypal in the cosmos of our American struggles. From the first, geographical accounts were called "journeys" and "journals," that is, places were translated into pieces of time, the extent of one day-lit day. The struggle of the Americas to throw off history and return to geography is one of the few common themes in all American cultures. Everywhere we can find the desire to free language, style, manners from the oppression of Europe's history in order to release the native voice of the land. That's why in the United States we elevate Whitman, and Faulkner and Hemingway, and Martin Luther King—to reassert the indigenous geography, the depth of place over the disease of time.

A fear of geography runs ever strong in the European for whom it must be civilized with roads and bridges, transformed into landscapes, pacified for vacations and possessed as property.

Remember Conrad's novel? What did Kurtz say from the bottom of his soul when he was plunged into the heart of darkness, utterly immersed in geographical terrain beyond the compass of European history: "The horror, the horror." Not Africa, slavery, exploitation and the socio-political explanation of "the problem" can account enough for Kurtz's despair. His is the cry of history when abandoned to geography.

A stain of blood streaks the documents of all America's history from Christian colonial times to the times of contemporary capitalism. The indigenous and environmental disasters, the extinction of languages, customs, songs, insects, birds, plants and animals, the rape, let us say, of geography by history shows the attempt of time to vanquish and harness place. The entire phenomenology of the vanquished and the oppressed—the suicidal stoicism, the stubborn passivity, the appeal of magic—can best be grasped as the resistance of geography to the violence of history.

The fear of geography, the panic that remains as a dormant God in the European imagination of nature—nature that must be climbed to the highest peak, the farthest pole, mapped and charted so that the demonic naturalness of geography is conquered by abstraction—is this "geographical panic" in face of the geographical immensity of the Hemisphere the untold root of this Hemisphere's violence? Is it our inability to face geography that drives the simple soldier and common settler into excesses of unspeakable violence, so ugly and cruel that they can be justified only by the highest authority, i.e., in the name of the Christian God?

Already in the seventeenth century, history's Age of Light, the New England forests were savagely cleared by the puritan settlers because in that dark and damp geography there lurked the unhealthy spirits of miasma and evil—and as well, the local pagan communities. Nathaniel Hawthorne exposes this fear of geography as a temptation to paganism, as does D. H. Lawrence later. Both hint that in the panic lives the ancient God Pan whom European history so dreads that it must be forever declaring him dead.

Geography was best served by the Romantics: For Humboldt it was inspirational, for Bonpland exhilarating, for Darwin instructional, and for Frederick Church, geography radiated the warm glow of love. The Romantics gave themselves over to place in their sketches and paintings, in their logbooks and narratives, in their exhaustive observations and collections. But then, this is to be expected since the Romantic spirit had already reverted to that devoted attention to geography known as Paganism. The meaning of "pagan," by the way, is rocky hillside. It is a word originating in the idea of being firmly set, of fixed place, implying a geographical dedication to each place, separate and distinct and belonging to the *spiritus loci* who inhabits it. How unlike the unifying monotheism of time which subjugates all phenomena with the same chain of events called history.

The moral of this preachment? If you would get out of history, get into geography.

On Confusing Culture with History: Let me try two definitions: civilization and culture. Civilization gets the job done, as best it can. Culture is song, the song that breaks out in the midst of the job. Culture pops up, sprouts in a petri dish. It is surprising, inexplicable, unpredictable—and largely unlearned. How strange that these spontaneous inventions startle and also feel necessary, as if it couldn't have been otherwise. How curious that an event can be utterly fresh and yet is greeted as part of the culture. Culture breaks into civilization, and yet is assimilated to it. Assimilation makes culture and civilization appear to be identical.

Because surprise, which means to be seized by the sudden, is a category of its own, a surprise is not merely something "new." The freshness is less a novelty than a blessing. To confuse novelty with spontaneity keeps us still within the framework of history, measuring the surprise against what was or already is. But a blessing is like grace; it just happens.

To believe history makes culture traps the soul in notions of development and in the belief that the past is a causally determining force. We then believe the past created the present, that we and everything around us are "results," eventually "victims." We then believe, further, that culture is defined by historical development—the development of music, of painting, schools of influence, tradition. History would make culture conditioned by contingencies, whereas I want to say that culture is governed by invisibles, the Gods, the Zeitgeist, the presence of the Other—a beloved, an audience, a group of friends, a dead master, a spirit—for whom the cultural act is presented as a gift. Civilization honors and maintains human achievements; culture gives them back to the Gods.

Historical antecedents need not be taken literally. They give a mythical ground to culture. They open the gates of fantasy. We fall back on the cave walls of Altamura, the red walls under the ashes of Pompeii, the library walls of Alexandria, or the ancient Andean Kingdoms. Culture needs images and figures apart from any immediate civilization, its time, its language. These historical antecedents, even if appealed to for authentication, imitated in style, and relied on for origination, are not so. They are rather evocations of alien spirits, required for incantational purposes, called upon to bless as a magic enhancement of a present project. It is not the past that gives a cultural work its validity.

Culture does require, however, rituals to aid its birth. These are not only the ones to do with skills: art school, music school. I am speaking now of the rituals of food and love, of conversations, civil necessities, places of opportunity in the midst of civilization where culture is invited to appear. These places may or may not be dinner parties, cafes, museums, theatres, or little magazines; these places where culture is invited may also be the streets, the taverns, the garages and dance halls. They do not require historical precedents so long as a kind of mythical impregnation of the atmosphere can be felt that sometimes is believed to descend into a place or a style from a historical personage—a great writer, a group of intellectuals, a public hero, an exceptional woman's originality. But this is fantasy, not history.

For this reason we must beware of academic institutions as cultural guardians, as if preservation of the dead and passing it forward to the young were the means of bringing culture to them. These institutions help civilize the young—or they may not, instead challenging them to rebel and dismember the dead and those who serve to keep them present. Such acts of destruction may be acts of culture challenging civilization.

We must also beware of the idea that culture is slow, that it takes wise ripenings, that it belongs to mustachioed elders who can quote aphorisms and to women who have traveled through many foreign lands and many bedrooms. The curio cabinet of collected mementos is not culture.

More likely, culture is made by the spirit often embodied by the young in its conflict with history. The young force the guardians of tradition to defend their accumulations ever more strongly, a reaction that maintains the civilization from generation to generation and justifies the reactionary conservatism of its defenders against the cultural incursions of jazz, boogie, rock, punk, salsa, rap, hip-hop, hardcore. Historians try to civilize these inventions by tracing their continuous evolution from basic common stems. They can account for everything except the surprise, the fresh departure from the basic stem. When history becomes the guide to culture we see the trace running through the variations, but never notice the unexpected. How account for the magic of change, the actual moment of culture breaking into the history of civilization?

The magic of change cannot be grasped by evolution. It does not show the epiphanic moment where one form becomes the next, the "missing" link—that hiatus where the surprises of the spirit, its inventions (in-venio = incomings) transform the same into the different. First three toes, then two; where is the connecting creature? How account for the magic of the first human to stand up tall? The smooth line of history is broken by the spontaneous interventions of the spirit. Magic makes culture. Or, as some argue, God in His Heaven intervening every microsecond.

The spectre who haunts the historical definition of culture is not senex as such; nor is it the senex fantasy of learnedness. Learning has an altogether different significance for culture. Rather than setting standards for accomplishments by measuring them against what has already been achieved, learning provides culture with inspiration and backing for courage to risk.

No, the worst spectre is the haunting urge of Progress. How many towns in the New World were named Progress, Hope, Liberty, Promise, Paradise, Eden, even Future, Deliverance, Redemption. Progress is merely an enthusiastic infusion of the emotion of Hope into Saturn's linear chain of historical continuity: History becomes Hope literalized.

In itself, continuity is merely a line from here to there, nothing better nothing worse, this then that, a series of contiguous moments, until the evil Hope appears. Then we have progress.

Once hope, longing, desire, regret—the full potency of what Freud called the "wish"—attaches itself to the chain of events, suddenly there are expectations and disappointments, the fantasies of progress and decline.

Culture has no need to get better, and so it cannot get worse. Magic fades; it loses luster; the trick no longer works. The song stops its singing. Like Hermes who suddenly was with us and just as suddenly vanishes. Here, say, in this or that city, among this crowd in the quarter, or around a university group a little theatre, there is a blossoming of culture; then it disappears to pop up somewhere else, among others. No progress; no decline. Appearance and disappearance. Celebration and mourning. When the God appeared there was hilaria; and when he disappeared, tristia. So it was with Dionysos.

In the animalized cosmos there is no progress either. Let's say you own a cat and keep your cat for seven or twelve years until one day it dies, stiff and straight on the floor. You get another cat, a different one, maybe a female one, and red. But there is no progress through the line of cats, or repetition of cats.

Memory makes comparisons among these avatars of the cat spirit; we see differences. But differences only become progress from better to worse or worse to better when differences are linked to history. For the native Plains peoples in what is now the United States, the buffalo that appeared each spring to eat the new grass after the snow were always the same buffalo roaring up out of the earth and disappearing at the end of the season as the snows came on again. Repetition. Differences and Sames—to use Aristotle's basic category; suddenness; changes; epiphanies—anything but progress.

Therefore a Foundation that aims to support culture will plant one foot firmly against history, against civilization in order to hold open a door to culture. It must welcome at its reception desk the apparitions that do not make historical sense, the appetitions that seem an abrupt break, without progenitors, something in and of itself without traces or sources, or with origins so remote they can only be imaginal.

Nor may a cultural Foundation build bridges that aid the assimilation of culture by civilization. The spirit does not use bridges; it prefers gaps so that is can leap. Nor will a cultural Foundation be occupied with renewal. New always implicates us in history. Instead, a Foundation will foster the pre-historical and a-historical, that a-civilized aspect of the soul which today we are calling the animal soul. Like the French painters sought the South Seas and African masks to get out of history, to defeat its civilizing influence. But not to get to "early Man" or "the origins of Art." No the appetite for primitivity seeks the utterly different, an alien beauty, like the display of the animal soul unadorned by civilization, archetypal in its constancy, and therefore not new but utterly familiar.

I am here echoing the voices of Lorca in regard to the Duende and Lautreamont in regard to the animal cry that is at the root of all poetic expression. "A need to animalize ... is at the origins of the imagination [whose] first function is to create animal forms." "In this universe the energy is aesthetic." [Cf. Gaston Bachelard's

Lautreamont.] The risks are great; for in this moment of the a-civilized, this moment of the animal soul, as Lautreamont and Bachelard have each said strongly we cannot tell creation from destruction. If creation is *ex nihilo*, out of nowhere, then the first step may be the creation of the *nihil*.

So this small society here, may find its historical traces back in Switzerland and Eranos, back in Romantic movements among friends in Germany and England, or back in associations of American artists and intellectuals in this Hemisphere—but these associations are not the source of what we do, providing no model, offering no guidance.

Rather we must imagine ourselves in a geography uninhabited except by the mythical figures who inhabit that geography. That's why the animal soul is so crucial in all our deliberations: only it can sniff out and know what is going on below the historical trappings we bring with us. Then we may imagine our activities and inventions unburdened by history, having progressed from nowhere, bearing no hopes, an absurdity, a free radical binding with no other molecule anywhere, for no practical end, no future, no historical significance, quite useless—and that we are definitely not making history even if we may be instigating culture by being together in this place and serving the ritual of this meeting.

IV. Return to the Animal

I magine that we let go of depending upon the new. To what then can the Americas turn to when facing the unknown— for American civilization always relies on Newness to mask its anxiety. What can nourish our optimism, our manic excitations that insist upon "explorations," "improvements," inventions" that must speak of this hemisphere as a "discovery?" What would happen to God, the Economy, and the frenzy of consumption from which this God lives, if the New were obliterated as a category: no new frontiers, no new fashions, new and improved products, diets, restaurants, no new generations of computers and cars, no newest state-of-the-art! No idea of the "latest." Without the New we would have dropped completely out of science and technology, out of economic development, personality growth. What would we then notice if we had no News? [*Ultima Noticias*] We would have fallen altogether through the supportive structure of history.

What remains below? Where does this fall take us? Into the pool of the ancestors, the eternal ones, the invisibles, waiting in the dreams, waiting in the melancholies, whispering still from childhood, like animal spirits, or animals themselves. They are not new. There are no new animals. Nor can we embrace the secret of their existence with such terms as repetition, eternal return, cyclical time, since these terms lead us back into history. The animal records no history and is therefore neither old nor new. Those fossil remains that establish its heredity, the carbon-dating of its bones, the paleozoology that reconstructs the milennial animal, are attempts to place this or that animal—the jaguar, the lizard, the monkey—into our scheme of time, into history again with traces of animal evolution. For the sake of what? The animal? No, so that we can be again at the top of the tree of time, the crown of creation.

So I make this turn to the animal for the sake of this Hemisphere, the reality of the world [*mondo*] when "*Nuevo*" is deleted as its qualifier. I am stripping this American world of its historical adjectives in an attempt to undo the cosmology inherent in the very style and order of our assembly here and now, this architecture, this schedule, the very syntax of the words and ideas as I stand here. Clearly, my attempt is absurd and will fail, but better absurdities, than conventions; better difficult failures than quick success.

The turn to the animal is an archetypal move when the mind has trapped itself into its own cages of thought. Aristotle—who gave us the scaffolding for all later European constructions in politics, ethics, logic, physics, poetics and metaphysics, the fields and disciplines of our institutions—Aristotle devoted three of every eight words to his study of animals. Yes, thirty-seven percent of his works concern animals. What fantasy did the animal carry for him? And Plato? In the midst of constructing his grand cosmology, the *Timaeus*, suddenly, while describing the geometric figure of the All, which includes the abstract shapes of the elements,

fire, earth, air and water, he states that there is a fifth, most compre-
hensive figure, a dodecahedron, a twelve-sided form which "had a
pattern of animal figures thereon." Already in his *Republic*, Plato there,
too, interrupts his dialectic with what seems like an absurd non-
sequitur, "the symbolic image of the soul" as a many-headed beast
with a ring of heads, tame and wild. Aristotle and Plato—I reverse
the usual order in order to escape the historical convention—must be
the Shamans of the European tradition in their turning to animals
for proposing the nature of the cosmos and of the soul.

This final and essential image of Plato's cosmology—strange,
unexpected, obscure as it may be—awards animals with cosmic
superiority. Plato's image suggests that mathematical abstraction
and elemental substances, i.e., theoretical physics, expressed by the
first four components, the elements, require something further: an
animation, an animalization. But Plato's animal image also indicates
that the mathematical and organic do not have to be divided, just
as God's instruction to Noah (Genesis 7:15-16) uses the exact
numerical language of architecture. In both cases, a single image
holds the abstract and the animated together.

Within an animalized cosmos, theories would not depart
from the actually palpable: we would have no hidden God, pure
Being, abstract truth, linguistic fundamentalism, symbolic logic,
unobservable particles as sufficient accounts—little physics and
less metaphysics. Yet, the Biblical ark is precisely measured in
cubits and the fifth essential shape in the *Timaeus* is a dodecahedron.

May we conclude that formal abstractions provide containing
shapes for animation? But that is all they are: houses for the
habitation of animals. Or, because form and animal are presented together in these ancient cosmologies, let us conclude
that the animal is structured, contained and law-abiding within
the inherent shapes of its specific species. This inherency of
cosmos (order) which self-limits animal life and is as eternal as
geometry, as surviving as the ark, psychology calls "instinct."

And yet, for all this profound recognition of the animal—as
ancestor who protects the soul and totem that maintains social
kinship; as dominant companion of the child's imagination and
play; as astral determinant of all cosmic events; as primordial source

of the impulse to make art of them on a cave wall and sing their sounds, dance their motions—yet for all this magical and shamanistic and philosophical appreciation, human opinion, to uphold its delusions of grandeur, continues to speak of the animal as "brute" and "beast," to curse other humans as dogs, pigs, rats, wolves and vultures, to identify the lower human soul of hungers, lusts, fears and greeds as "animal." In the popular science of television, we are taught to see the animal as example of predator, competitor, territorial warfare, gender domination, hierarchical order—a media reflection of the capitalist self disguised as nature education.

Of the many attempts to seize the essence of animal being in a net of human concepts, "pinned and wriggling on the wall" (T. S. Eliot), of all the derogatory comparisons between human and animal that keeps a cut between us so that the human may keep faith with its own dissociation, the most apparent and necessary characteristic has escaped our cleverness. This characteristic is animal display. All animal life *shows*; it has visible exteriority, whether skin, coat, feathers, scales, or even the thinnest membrane of simple life-forms. Adolf Portmann, the eminent Swiss zoologist (who was, among all his renowned accomplishments, also the guiding spirit of the Eranos Foundation for thirty years) wrote: "Appearance like experience is a basic characteristic of living beings...". All living things are urged to present themselves, display themselves, to show, *ostentatio*, which was a usual Latin translation of the Greek *phantasia*, fantasy. Each animal's ostentation is its fantasy of itself, its self-image as an aesthetic event without ulterior function. Portmann brought many kinds of evidence for these "unaddressed appearances." For example: the small transparent oceanic creatures living in the interiors of other larger creatures or below the depths where light can reach or having no visual organs themselves, and so whose brilliantly vivid and symmetrically patterned forms serve no functions—neither as messages to their own species, as attractions, as warnings, or disguises.

It is sufficient just to display. Display is fundamental to animal life and this is the first lesson the animal teaches. The animal continually reminds that the play of creation is revelation. To be is to be seen; beauty is given with existence. As Portmann

shows, to be seen is as genetic as to see: the organic structures of
patterning, coloring and symmetrical display are as genetic as
the ocular organs that allow seeing the display. In fact, the coat is
ontogenetically prior to the eye that sees the coat. It is this beauty
of the phenomenal and its everlasting return of the same that the
animals reveal, as if they revel in their own fantasy—not information, not
communication, not metaphor, beyond understanding and meaning,
the beauty of these amazingly complicated and "other" living beings.
It is as if they say: Respect us—re-spect, which means, "look again."

    And what then do we see, once we open our own animal eye?
We see, says Portmann, sheer appearance for its own sake. Display
not directed at anything, anyone, or what he terms "Unaddressed
appearances." "*Die Erscheinung ist ihr eigener Zweck*"—the self-
presentation of the animal is its own end, and its color and shape
and pattern, he says, is the work of very specific biological structures.

    Does this not say that the animal is above all an aesthetic
creation, that an animal eye sees first of all the display of beauty,
and that the animal is compelled by instinctual necessity to present
itself as an image? Portmann's radical insight into the biological
necessity of the aesthetic explodes the sheerly functional notion
of animals, struggling to feed and breed, ever in fear and trembling.
It also explodes the silly, lightweight, decorative notions of
aesthetics; instead "show" is laid down in basic structure of
biological life. Biology itself insists on aesthetic display.

    The animal opens not only into the flesh of life but also
towards the Gods. According to legends and rituals worldwide,
animals impart the secrets of the cosmos. They are instructors in
cosmology, that is, they mediate between the Gods and humans;
they have divine knowledge. In polytheistic cultures they are
themselves divinities. For ancient Egyptians, according to Henri
Frankfort, animals were divine because of "their inarticulate wisdom,
their certainty, their unhesitating achievement, and above all their
static reality. With animals the continual succession of generations
brought no change ... They would appear to share...the fundamental
nature of creation," its repetitious, rhythmic stability.

    For indigenous peoples from Amazonas to far Northern
latitudes, for whom animals display the divine, an animal is an

eternal form walking around, the palpable presence of the regeneration of time, of adapting and surviving life—an immortality utterly of this world, this world its Eden, needing no elsewhere, and no ecstasies. No Being guarantees its existence; its existence guarantees being. Each animal is eternity sensuously displayed, and so the stars, most enduring of all images, were imagined with animal names. For this animal certainty and unchanging reality, psychology, as I said, has invented the term "instinct."

Instinct, too, ignores progress and the New. It knows no problems. It has no notion of history. And so, moralist philosophers often declare instinct the enemy of civilization. They assert that the continuity and certainty below the human will and its civilization belong to a lesser kingdom. Long before actual animals in the seas and the jungles vanish, much philosophy continues to authorize extinction by an ontological definition of animal as soulless, irrational, mechanistic. All the while, this same position does admit that the animal's basic instinct is continuity, i.e., the "preservation of the species," thereby affirming that the animal is the unhesitating answer to nihilism. It must go on, each according to its kind in its eternal repetitive displays. Each animal recapitulates the survival of the Ark and the original Garden.

V. Shaman: A Human Animal

Mircea Eliade, in his complete, pioneering, and extraordinary study of shamanism, observed that the shaman has a special relation with the animal kingdom. He (or she) heals by means of animal potencies, speaks directly with animals, masters them, takes on animal forms, and often bears an animal name. Part of his initiation is the special interfusion of his powers with the power of the founding totem animal of the tribe or clan.

Our narrowly humanistic anthropology conceives the animal aspect of the shaman as his (or her) possession by spirit-powers so that the human form becomes mimetic to a jaguar, a tiger, a bear, an eagle, hawk, snake, etc. The human imitates and identifies with the animal and can enact its nature.

Now, what if we reverse our cosmology so that the human does not come first? Then, perhaps, that horned shaman dancer-image on the paleolithic cave-wall, and all the animals since who accompany the shaman in so many societies, would be prior to the human. Then "possession," "imitation," "identification" and "enactment" would not be the right terms. Then the shaman is the actual incarnation of an animal spirit, an animal image in human form, and not a human at all, or at least not altogether human. Rather than think the human is enacting the bear, it is the bear appearing as a human, as tribal accounts report. The physical animal and the corporal shaman share a common bear image, so of course they communicate. They are imbued by the same spirit that is neither human nor animal, and both. The shaman is that particular human who acts as plenipotentiary representative of the animal kingdom, endowed with the animal's wisdom, its ferocity, its inhumanity and yet strange caring regard for the human, and its rectitude—and hence the shaman's capacity to "heal," i.e., set things straight and put them on the right path.

These animal presences appear nightly in our urban dreams. As invitations of the image, they can lead us out of our human confinement, bringing wisdom, ferocity, detachment and healing. We are each lesser shamans, shamans of a minor magnitude, in our receptivity to the animal presences that come to our dreams. These presences also bless our peculiarities—our serpentine wiles, our aquiline rapaciousness, the smothering clutch of our bear-ish hugs. Their images provide an imaginative backing to human pathologies and traits—fishy, mousey, piggish, crabby, ratty, wolfish, weaselly, cocky, foxy. They remain beautifully independent of our interpretations which attempt to cage them within our subjectivity as bits of our selves, as impulses, instincts, appetites, fears, complexes, mothers, fathers, sisters, brothers, and sexual fantasies.

The first sign of shamanistic power, according to Joseph Campbell, is hearing song. Song as the breaking in of the invisible; song as vision. The animal translates its presence into the human shape by means of vocal display; lyric, chant, melody, poem. The

child, relapsing into the primeval forest of penumbral uncon-
sciousness, needs to be sung to sleep or sings in its sleep. The
Orphic voice spans the gap, holds the rhythmic tension between
human and animal.

Earlier we referred to Joseph Conrad's Kurtz as the representative
of history succumbing to geography as horror. "All Europe," says
Conrad, "contributed to the making of Kurtz." But something else
unmade him, for, "Whatever he was, he was not common. He had
the power to charm or frighten rudimentary souls into an aggravated
witchdance in his honor...". The signal trait of Kurtz was: "A voice.
He was little more than a voice." "Of all his gifts the one that
stood out preeminently, that carried with it a sense of real presence,
was his ability to talk, his words—the gist of expression, the
bewildering, illuminating, the most exalted and the most contemptible, the pulsating stream of light or the deceitful flow from
the heart of an impenetrable darkness." (Chapter Two)

As Kurtz disintegrates, his talk becomes ever more strange and
wild. From the viewpoint of the European colonizer, he was going
mad; from the viewpoint of the primordial geography he was
reverting to the earth (a word Conrad uses again and again) and
becoming the voice of it. He was "adored" by his natives. "His
ascendancy was extraordinary.... Chiefs came everyday to see him.
They would crawl." "He had taken a high seat among the devils of
the land ... I mean literally ... to preside at certain midnight dances
ending with unspeakable rites, which ... were offered up to him."
One disciple repeats: "He made me see things." "He enlarged my
mind." "You ought to have heard him recite poetry—his own
too....Poetry!" And the images of him are phantomlike: his head,
bald as an ivory ball; "He looked at least seven feet long." (Chapter
Three) The fascinating power he held, the rites he presided over,
the mantic poetic speech, the range of mind, the weird appearance—
the disintegration. Was it madness; was it initiation? In short, was
Kurtz not only a colonial but also a shaman? And was "the horror" a last repenting insight into the colonial by the shaman, into
the human heart by the animal vision?

VI. Penultimate

The return to the animal has been urged on us by every sort of ideological bestiary, the primitivists, the Rousseauian Romantics, the primal therapists, the shaman-guiders, the liberationists, and by those who have just found the wolf, running with them or dancing with them, and we are further urged to save all animals by abstaining from leather and fur, meat and tallow, eggs and milk, and to use no medicine that might save our lives because it has cost an animal's.

All of this noble. Yet all of this is symptomatic of the marvelously unconscious tendency to literalize. I mean that urgency to fix in the concrete physical world what has gone astray in the symbolic metaphysical world. Once again: animal becomes a physical problem when the animal is failed by the metaphysical imagination.

Now that we have recognized that the essence of animal display—for that is how we distinguish their kinds, name them, classify them, as Adam did when the species paraded before him in Eden and he could see their names, and as Noah did when he had them come two by two according to their different kinds—then the question which follows is: In what manner do we, as human animals, display our essence? What is the essential self-presentation of the human species?

It can hardly be our skins, our mating dances, our posterior exposures, or threatening gestures. These are like other creatures. Anthropologists who study humanoid history find certain traits distinctive to humans—but these too are questionable, because birds make collections of small beautiful objects; insects construct homes; lions collaborate; ants have social organizations; elephants remember the dead; dogs mourn; squirrels plan ahead; horses take instruction; cows respond to music; migrating fish remember; birds read the stars; chimpanzees learn words; and many species use tools. Besides, our question asks not the usual one: "How do humans differ from animals?" We are asking: "What is the specific human form of animal display? How have we, like animals, a particularly characteristic mode of self-presentation?

There is one answer, I believe, that takes care of both sorts of question: What is different in the human species, and what is the most characteristically human kind of display? That answer is speech. Only we have the palate, tongue, epiglottis, larynx, pharynx arrangement that permits articulation. Sounds, melody, rhythm, communication, imitation, symbol systems, yes, many animals have these elaborations, but not rhetorical speech.

The signal mark of "wolf children," that is, those raised in the wild by animals or deprived of all human contact in early years, would seem to be their rhetorical disability. Not merely eating with mouth and hands, absence of toilet training, or postural deformities, but speech turns out to be their most damaged instinct. The humanization of the wolf-child, in fact, the incorporation of any alien (barbarian in the Greek sense), or voice-afflicted person requires the learning of rhetorical skills. By this I mean not merely language for communication, expression, socialization or literacy. It is more than functional use; it is to regain the primordial basis of human nature.

By means of speech we enact what animals do in behavior. With speech we warn, claim territory, challenge and destroy. With speech we court and seduce a mate, and by means of speech we instruct our offspring and organize our group disciplines. The primacy of the word is confirmed by what our civilization considers its holiest text which states clearly, "In the beginning was the word." And this word was imagined, let us remember, not as making order or providing meaning, but as the display of light, the ostentation of a divine radiance.

VII. Terminus of the Interminable

At the end now I ask myself in your behalf what has been happening here? What indeed have you all been listening to? And your listening has been superb—gracious, generous, willing. So it is time to review what we have been doing. Certainly no problems were solved. And certainly nothing new was presented. We have not helped with the dilemmas of The Economy, or saved the environment. Nor has oppression been lifted, or history made. Neither has a psychology been elaborated.

Two themes of those touched upon do, however, remain, the theme of Culture and the theme of Animals. So it is the duty of the speaker at the end to close the gestalt by bringing the only two remnants of a generally destructive engagement together. I am obliged to show a connection between culture and animal.

We may build this connection very simply upon the premise that speech is the specific display of the human animal. I would here both narrow and expand the term "speech," on the one hand, to exclude the signals of ordinary communication and information which can be relegated to symbol systems, gestures, and electronic devices; on the other hand, to include song, poem, oration, incantation, speculation—in short rhetorical display in a variety of forms.

I am saying that care with speech is the human way of preserving the animal, our way of self-preservation. I am saying that devotion to rhetoric becomes a primordial human task because it is the essence of our animal nature. This dedication to speech was a characteristic noted first in this Hemisphere among the natives of Tierra del Fuego whom, it was observed by early visitors from Europe, lived in most primitive conditions—exposed to endless cold rain with minimal shelter, a poverty of tools and food, and yet had the most astounding vocabulary and tradition of fables, tales, stories. Living "like animals," as the observers may have noted—indeed, living the human animal's primordial necessity of rhetoric.

The specific essence of human display cannot be the image. Animals, too, are images. Even if C. G. Jung declared that psyche is image, psyche is not confined to humans. Animals, too, display their images and, in the narrower sense of the word, animals also "imagine"—as the dog kicks and growls in its sleep, the spider finds precisely that corner to spin its web, the cat suddenly leaps into a capricious game with its own tail. Image and imagining are shared by humans and animals, but not speech.

To clarify the role of image, let us say that the image is at the aesthetic core of all animation. It is what makes life displayed, i.e., aesthetic. Even plants and stones have a *causa formalis*, a quiddity, those particular patternings which make each thing what it is and different from every other. However, the articulation of the image, the rhetorical elaboration, the translation into word, gesture, syntax, symbol, thought, lyric, rhyme—the poiesis that makes the human into *homo faber*—that is specific only to us.

I am declaring a duty to the animal drive to sing, to speak up and speak out, to declaim, confabulate, expostulate, gesticulate, persuade, cajole, deprecate, blaspheme, woo and insult. By these means instinct is satisfied as much as by any meal, any bed, any infant. When we perform these acts we are true to our animal selves and when we fail this display human nature withers and culture evaporates. George Orwell in his *1984* already noted the threat to culture by the shrinking of speech: "Every concept that can ever be needed will be expressed by exactly one word, with its meaning rigidly defined and all its subsidiary meanings rubbed out ... Every year fewer and fewer words, and the range of consciousness always a little smaller."

The narrowing of words to single definitions and the narrowing of vocabulary is only part of it. More significant is the inhibition of rhetorical display, the fundamental disbelief in the magical trans-substantive power of poesis to make reality, which then reduces the idea of reality to the language of stupidity: acronyms, numbers, instructions, sound-bites, slogans, ads, one-liners, package contents, charts, data. It's all in the data-bank, except the sudden song. The murder of speech is the self-murder of the human animal, a suicidal evisceration of our species' specific endowment. Like tigers losing their stripes, like beached whales and blind eagles are we without our rhetoric. Speech is our body, speech is our shape, speech is our beauty.

The restoration of the cosmic imagination to the vision of those shamans, Plato and Aristotle, the preservation of the human species, and the gift of culture—all come down to the elevation of rhetoric to prime place. For this reason—for now I am literally at an end—the return to the animal means a return to the poetic urge in any citizen, an urge symbolized by the actual poet who, like an alpha animal, leads the herd with the power of display. And, we have ended in this room in a poetic ecology in the presence of these human animals, poets, whose abilities are even more blessed by the Spanish tongue.

THE AMERICAN DISCOVERY:
MISTAKES AND FICTIONS

JAY LIVERNOIS

The contemporary and popular fictions of the "Discovery of America" and its resultant history has been based on repressed and suppressed ideas and facts; or what can be called—as seen from a certain perspective—mistakes. For example, Columbus did not and could not believe he had run into a "New World."

We know that Columbus' "heroic" voyage of exploration was primarily a commercial project. His main financial backers were Queen Isabella and King Ferdinand of Spain and the Genoese and Florentine (Medici)[1] banks.[2] But what is often neglected and unstated is that Columbus embarked on his first and subsequent voyages with a pious yet apocalyptic goal which had as its origins the medieval dream of religious and military Crusade. This goal was to find a short route to the riches of the Indies so that he, the self-proclaimed mystical pilot of Christ, *Christoferens*,[3] could finance a new crusade for Alexander VI, the Spanish Borgia Pope, and Ferdinand and Isabella of Spain. The crusade was to be a

Jay Livernois is working on a new translation of Petrarch's *On Solitude*. A version of this paper was presented at the Myth and Theatre Festival in Villneuve-lez-Avignon, France, in 1995.

continuation and expansion of the *reconquista* lately brought to conclusion in Granada on the Iberian peninsula but was now to have as its goal the recapture of the Holy Sepulcher in Jerusalem.[4] Columbus believed that when the Holy Sepulcher was captured by Christian knights under the direction of the Spanish monarchs, all the world's peoples would gather at Mount Zion, and the world would come to an end. In an incredible document called the *Book of Prophecies* (written after his third voyage), he outlined the belief that he was chosen by God to bring this about through his explorations.

When Columbus sailed into what other Europeans sensed and then recognized as the utterly new Caribbean basin, he could only interpret what he found by what he needed and wanted to find,[5] literally the spice island *Indies*, naming the people he met there *Indians*. He clearly skewed his geographical calculations (as many scholars have now authenticated) so he could realistically and scientifically convince himself that he had come onto the fabled islands of riches just off the coast of Japan or China. He had to convince himself of this because he believed he was divinely chosen to find the wealth of the Orient by going west. He wrote in his *Book of Prophecies* that neither reason nor math nor maps had enabled him to succeed in discovering these new islands for Spain. Instead he firmly believed that it had been determined by God's will.[6] Here, believing is not only seeing and doing but also calculating.

But almost from the moment of discovery, the Caribbean islands did not seem about to produce a treasure of spices and gold. These after all were the quick, easy, familiar capital commodities Columbus needed to finance not only his medieval dream of a Christian Crusade[7] aimed at recapturing Jerusalem but also to pay off the creditors for his voyage. He therefore immediately enslaved the *Indians* and hoped to use this commodity to raise money on his return to Spain. He was familiar with slavery (and the gold trade) from the days when he worked for the Portuguese in their West African trading and colonial ventures based as they were on this black and yellow lucre.[8] Hence the archetypal raw voyage of exploration and the ideal of Christian conversion of newly discovered peoples became a voyage of cruel human exploitation. It all happened, perhaps, in an unreflective blink of Columbus' monotheistic mind, a mind seemingly blind but yet filled with Christian Righteousness and driven by a millenarian apocalyptic vision. This point has not been made enough by historians because the image of Columbus as a religious fanatic does not sit well with the image of Columbus as a Renaissance man of reason and science. However, Columbus' extreme medieval piety, which was always attested to by his contemporaries, has now been confirmed by the discovery of this *Book of Prophecies*.

Columbus had an imaginative obtuseness and ambitious single-mindedness[9] stemming from these medieval apocalyptic fantasies. He was not a man of the Renaissance, not even of the Inquisition, that Holy institution which plagued Renaissance Spain. This perhaps accounts for the strange history of his obscurity in Renaissance Europe and his rediscovery only late into the eighteenth century when his image became useful for American revolutionary propaganda. This early obscurity led to the odd fact that the new world Columbus mistakenly "found" came to be named in his lifetime not "Columbia" but "America." As most people know, America was named after the Renaissance Florentine, Amerigo Vespucci, whose imagination, unlike Columbus,' was not bound up by medieval piety and grandiose dreams of Crusades. Vespucci's imagination was more receptive to the Renaissance. His Florentine culture and education had given him the ability to see and imagine a "new world." Consequently America was rightfully named for Vespucci as he was the first to understand that the land run into by Columbus was completely new and different from what was already known. Vespucci wrote that:

> In the past I have written to you in rather ample detail about my return from those new regions which we searched for and discovered with the fleet, at the expense and orders of His Most Serene Highness the King of Portugal, and which can be called a new world, since our ancestors had no knowledge of them and they are entirely new matter to those who hear about them. Indeed, it surpasses the opinion of our ancient authorities, since most of them assert that there is no continent south of the equator, but merely that sea which they called

the Atlantic; furthermore, if any of them did affirm that a continent was there, they gave many arguments to deny that it was habitable land. But this last voyage of mine has demonstrated that this opinion of theirs is false and contradicts all truth, since I have discovered a continent in those southern regions that is inhabited by more numerous peoples and animals than in our Europe, or Asia or Africa, and in addition I found a more temperate and pleasant climate than in any other region known to us, as you will learn from what follows, where we shall briefly write only of the main points of the matter, and of those things more worthy of note and record, which I either saw or heard in this new world, as will be evident below.[10]

The realization that this was a discovery of new world continents (and not just ocean rutted islands) was electric from Vespucci's Renaissance perspective, grounded as it was in the fifteenth century's re-discovery by humanists of the "old world;" the Renaissance, after all, was a rebirth of the long-suppressed and Christian-occluded classical pagan world. Of course Vespucci in his enthusiastic letters on the marvels of the new world[11] could not see how this *Mundus Novus* was to change with European contact (of which he was an important part). But it was certainly to radically change Europe and the European imagination with a New World's vast, continental "newness," and Vespucci was clearly the first to recognize this "newness." Analysts would say Columbus was "in denial." For years he denied America's "newness" even as he discovered, explored, and saw it.

This "newness" was a shock that was to last for centuries, and in fact seems to continue to shock and surprise the European or Eurocentric imagination. Europeans still get the American psyche wrong. Much has recently been written and speculated about the "American" influence on Europeans who explored this *Novus Mundus* and stayed.[12] For the most part this has been from a Eurocentric point of view even when written by American scholars. It is the view that the "American" influence on Europeans is morally, spiritually, culturally, and even physically bad.[13]

Ironically, the Eurocentric point of view[14] progressed absurdly in the eighteenth century to a "scientific" and philosophical belief that everything found in nature in America—plants, animals, land, people—was biologically inferior and therefore inherently less than European "originals." One of the great proponents of this idea was the popular French naturalist Georges-Louis Leclerc de Buffon (1707-1788),[15] who wrote, referring to his belief in America's decided inferiority to the Old World, that this was the "greatest fact, the most general, the least known to all naturalists before me."[16]

Many Europeans following this line of thought concluded that all of America's environment was decidedly inferior to Europe's.[17] In Europe it was feared that an "American" process of degeneracy leading to inferiority and untrustworthiness started by being born in America, even if the parents were from "pure" European stock.[18] What can we assume but that, embedded in what appears to be this European fear of the "American," is also a fear of loss of control of the "other" by Europeans and their respective governments, whether that "other" is indigenous or of European descent or is a transplanted European.[19]

Perhaps this fear occurs as a reaction to the effect of vast horizontal space and the great distance between Europe and the two larger American continents.[20] But additionally, starting with Columbus, the fear on the part of European governments (in this case the royal government of Ferdinand and Isabella of Spain) was that any new lands discovered could be easily detached from out of their control by "servants" (such as Columbus), and then these "servants" could set themselves up as rulers of an independent country. Throughout the fourteenth and fifthteenth centuries in Italy, *condottiere* (mercenary warlords) often seized power in the city states that hired them. Milan was particularly vexed by this problem, and Venice was always on her guard against it. Just a few hundred years previously at the start of the 12th century, the French Count Henry of Burgundy (who was in the employ of the Kingdom of Leon as a *conquistador*) seized the recently conquered county of Portugal and declared his independence from the Kingdoms of Castille and Leon. He then went to war against both Moors and Christians to secure the county's autonomy. This resulted in the founding and establishment of the Iberian rival kingdom of Portugal.

Much of Columbus' troubled history was based on the Spanish government's fear that the proclaimed "Admiral of the Ocean Sea" had an agenda to carve out a hereditary viceroyship for himself out of the lands he discovered. The hard contract Columbus negotiated with the Spanish sovereigns before he set out on his first voyage can be read as possibly preparing the way for a hereditary kingdom for his family in any newly discovered lands. And by 1494 Columbus, as Governor of the Indies, was indeed acting like an Andalusian grandee. This set off his royal patrons' distrust of him. It seemed to them that he could not be controlled because of distance and temperament, and this was seen as setting a bad precedent.

The act that almost certainly triggered Columbus' recall to Spain in chains by Ferdinand and Isabella was his bestowal of five hundred and fifty indigenous Taino[21] Indians on colonists returning to Spain from Hispaniola. With this gesture Columbus abrogated to himself the right of creating serfs (and therefore wealth) which was until then one of the feudal prerogatives of the rulers of Spain within Spanish possessions. When Queen Isabella heard of Columbus' actions, she lashed out with, "By virtue of what *power* does my own Admiral give away my own *vassals* to anyone at all?"[22] Isabella's royal anger was caused by her fear of loss of power to Columbus in the recently acquired lands, as he was taking and dispensing what she saw as her feudal vassals (and hence wealth). Isabella's anger was not caused by her worry over the Indians, their treatment, and consequent lack of conversion. Her anger had to do with her sense of having a prerogative of power abrogated—medieval vassalage (and its potential revenues)— and not with any humane concern for the enslavement of Indians or their religious state.

This outward intention of trying to maintain control of others and themselves when faced with the shock of the American "other" and its "newness" was done, I believe, to preserve, however knowingly or unknowingly, a European self and psyche. Of course this European attempt at unity of psyche and control eventually failed, not for lack of trying or will, or even because of the sheer size of America, its space,[23] and its unusually large landscape of horizontal openness. It was probably America's newness that slowly

wore down the systems of physical and imaginative control brought
with European explorers, capitalists, and colonists. The result,
after just one or two generations of Europeans in a New World
context, was a novel type of culture, person, and imagination—a
new kind of soul. But always from the European perspective it was
a bastardized Europeanism, caused by an alien nature to be degenerate, savage, disfavored, and monstrous—called "American" with all
of the cultural insecurity that that name still carries. The European
distortion of the American narrative ranges far beyond the "discovery" accounts and can be seen even at work in the attitude
of the New England Puritans as they confronted "America." And it
is, I contend, still at work today.

This culturally inferior and insecure "Americanism" still
dominates much of the fantasy about America. European intellectuals, like the contemporary English writer Kathleen Raine, are all
too typical, disdainfully claiming that America "lacks a unity
of culture."[24] It can be found as well in Americans who have come
to identify themselves with European culture.[25]

A way to get out of this psychological bind of being totally
dominated by European culture was to set up an imaginative
construct which differentiated America from Europe but clung
to a familiar collective fiction giving it the form of a unified
narrative vision. A cliché example is how America can be seen
from foreign shores—perhaps more than ever—as the land of
golden opportunity. It is almost a prerequisite for Europeans to
project this onto America to perceive America in any positive light.
This often results, however, in a disdain of America changing
to an undifferentiated blind adoration. Yet the disdain, it should
be noted, is always there, even when suppressed under adoration,
and the two are often knowingly tied together.

For Europeans to have been able to dominate America,
especially after it was realized that what was discovered was not
just different groups of islands further out in the Ocean Sea or
off the coasts of Japan or China[26] but continental land masses
north and south of the Caribbean Sea, it became necessary to set
up fictions differentiating America from Europe. The chief
collective fiction that was developed and then projected on America

was a vision of America as a "wilderness," possessing a corresponding Neolithic "primitiveness" and "savagery" which we now know became Europe's overt burden to civilize but covert opportunity to exploit. Strangely, to this day the idea of "wilderness" has come to us almost unquestioned and is still central to the myth of America's historical discovery, settlement, development, and literary narrative. It is especially true of the founding myth of Puritan New England.

In mentioning Puritan New England in the context of America, Harvard's Perry Miller's re-discovery of the Puritan narrative and the resulting modern flood of interest in Puritan studies must be considered. This fascination and near obsession with Puritan studies[27] (framed as they are in the "wilderness" and "primitive" fantasy of New England), comes from what could be called a dream of origins. Perry Miller, with his bold, romantic, and adventurous confession in the preface to *Errand into the Wilderness* (his seminal collection of essays on the Puritans), plucked the archetypal chord of origins, although always in his persona as a romantic tough guy and academic Hemingway.[28] He writes,

> These papers, along with three or four books, are all I have yet been able to realize of a determination conceived three decades ago at Matadi on the banks of the Congo. I came there seeking "adventure," jealous of older contemporaries to whom that boon had been offered by the First World War.... The adventures that Africa afforded were tawdry enough, but it became the setting for a sudden epiphany (if the word be not too strong) of the pressing necessity for expounding my America to the twentieth century.

> To bring into conjunction a minute event in the history of historiography with a great one: it was given to Edward Gibbon to sit disconsolate amid the ruins of the Capitol at Rome, and to have thrust upon him the "laborious work" of *The Decline and Fall* while listening to barefooted friars chanting responses in the former temple of Jupiter. It was given to me, equally disconsolate on the edge of a jungle of central Africa, to have thrust upon me the mission of expounding what I took to be the innermost propulsion of the United States, while supervising, in that

barbaric tropic, the unloading of drums of case oil flowing out
of the inexhaustible wilderness of America.[29]

In Miller's "sudden epiphany" that sets him on his life's mission,
he conflates his fantasy of American "wilderness" with the African
"barbaric tropic" that was surrounding him while in the belgian
Congo in the 1920's. His vision of like wildernesses made him
curious about the beginnings of the United States. This meant
diving into the Puritans, their writings, and particularly their
metaphorical "erand into the wilderness," an overall subject
area his graduate professors at Harvard assured him held nothing
of any interest for a possible career in the academy.

But in all of Miller's writings, it is striking that he never
questions whether this wilderness of the Puritans actually existed,
any more than he would question the barbaric tropic he experienced
literally as an adventurous young man. He seems to have believed
in the Puritans and their literal truth just as the Puritans believed
in the literal truth of a transcendent God and the *Bible*. It is strange
that Miller, an atheist and existentialist, should not have been
more skeptical of the underlying "wilderness" paradigm which
informed how the Puritans thought and acted. It is true that all
the critical and historical writings he worked with believed in the
rightness of the early founders' accounts of what they had to
contend with in planting a colony. For example, Frederick Jackson
Turner's thesis of the importance of the forest and frontier in
shaping America was not criticized in its essence by Miller; he
dismissed it because he, Miller, was not a formalist who believed
that a form—in this case the forest—determined American reality.
Miller does not question Turner's belief in the literal existence
of the forest (or in Miller's way of thinking, the wilderness) and the
role it played. He says, "Happily we no longer are obliged to
believe this, although we are ready to recognize, thanks to Turner,
that unless we acknowledge the existence of the forest the character of
American history is obscure."[30] I contend that the role of the
forest or wilderness, even if only as a figure of speech, should not
be taken unquestioningly as a condition of how a narrative should
be interpreted.

Miller would not like this critical position, nor would the Puritans themselves. But my point with both Miller's and the Puritans' "wilderness" fiction is that it was necessary for them to use this fiction to psychologically preserve a kind of monovision and focus for what they were doing. Otherwise the "other" of New England would have overwhelmed their errand and led to a kind of collapse right at the beginning of both their projects—the Puritans' in their founding, and of Miller's in his founding scholarship. For Miller, no matter how much he protests that he does not believe in the Puritans' beliefs, ultimately he needs them, and his influence and success in American studies perhaps testifies to the rightness of his intuitive use of them. But let's look at what the Pilgrims' (or Separatists') said their reactions to America were, and what they said about the so-called "wilderness" they found when they first came to New England.

The Pilgrims arrived at Cape Cod in late autumn of 1620. Six weeks after their arrival, they were still trying to decide where the best place was to land and found a settlement. While her husband, the soon to be Governor William Bradford, was out exploring the Cape, Dorothy Bradford threw herself overboard and drowned. This suicide, although mostly hushed up through history, was evidently brought on by a collective depression which had overcome the "tenderhearted women who came to New England among the pioneers, that their hearts grew faint and sick when they first beheld that wild-looking northern land, so different from the green and cultivated England they had left."[31] So it seems the first traumatic, yet then suppressed act for the Plymouth Plantation was a suicide brought on by despair from this "wild-looking northern land." Evidently faced with the new, and what had to be for their *errand*, "wild-looking" America, the first group of English (but soon to be American) women were terrified.

The earliest and most authoritative narrative we have of how these first English Europeans perceived the new world of New England comes from this same William Bradford, the Plymouth Colony's longtime governor and unfortunate husband of Dorothy. *Of Plymouth Plantation* by "the Sometime Governor thereof" (as

Bradford referred to himself on the manuscript's cover page),
although composed between 1630 and 1650, was not published
until 1856. But it was referred to and used by colonial historians,
from Nathaniel Morton to Increase Mather and his son, Cotton,
and also by William Hubbard.[32] People *knew* it and used it, so its
influence was felt indirectly. In it Bradford recorded his remembered
but collective first impressions of the new world of New England.
He writes,

> Besides, what could they see but a hideous and desolate wilder-
> ness, full of wild beasts and wild men—and what multitudes there
> might be of them they knew not. Neither could they, as it were,
> go up to the top of Pisgah to view from this wilderness a more
> goodly country to feed their hopes; for which way soever they
> turned their eyes (save upward to the heavens) they could have
> little solace or content in respect of any outward objects. For
> summer being done, all things stand upon them with a weather-
> beaten face, and the whole country, full of woods and thickets,
> represented a wild and savage hue.[33]

Clearly Bradford sees New England as a "desolate wilderness, full of
wild beasts and wild men," and anthropomorphizes it giving it "a
weather-beaten face" with "a wild and savage hue."

Bradford ends the narrative of chapter IX, *Their Voyage and
Safe Arrival at Cape Cod*, with (adapted) quotes from the *Bible* which
are now famous because of their heroic and historic resonance.
In Bradford's immortal words,

> May not and ought not the children of these fathers rightly say:
> "Our fathers were Englishmen which came over this great ocean,
> and were ready to perish in this wilderness; but they cried unto
> the Lord, and He heard their voice and looked on their adver-
> sity," etc. ". . . When they wandered in the desert wilderness out
> of the way, and found no city to dwell in, both hungry and thirsty,
> their soul was overwhelmed in them."[34]

Bradford's use of the Biblical wilderness to explain and understand what he is seeing in this new world is crucial. The
"other" of the new New England landscape is perceived to be
wilderness, but a wilderness as understood through his understanding

of the *Bible*. This of course leads to the direct although subtle identification of the Pilgrims with the Hebrews throughout Bradford's narrative, and probably it would be right to assume he imagined it that way while he lived.

Therefore the whole enterprise of founding Plymouth, a narrative written down years after the fact by Bradford, as is well known, was caught up in and couched in the heroic Biblical myth of *Exodus*. This myth and narrative fiction was a kind of archaic and deliberately backward looking Hebraic pastoral which was adopted by all of Puritan (and then Protestant) New England. Ironically it is what drove forward New England's plantation and business enterprises psychologically and enabled them to maintain (with the help of periodic renewals) a unity of self and culture in the face of psychological fears, collapses, and the terrors of the "other," often continental in size. However the strangeness of new soul faced by soon to become "new" Americans was sometimes so overpowering that a watery death (and receiving a suicide's eternal damnation) looked better.

Notes

[1] John Noble Wilford, *The Mysterious History of Columbus: An Exploration of the Man, the Myth, the Legacy*, (New York: Knopf, 1992), 94-95.

[2] *Letters from a New World: Amerigo Vespucci's Discovery of America*, ed. and intro. Luciano Formisano, foreword Garry Wills, trans. David Jacobson, (New York: Marsilio, 1992), xxv.

[3] Wilford, 226, 229.

[4] Wilford, 230.

[5] This was further reinforced by the fact that Columbus had no experts or specialists on his ships. He did not even have a slight chance of knowing or guessing at what the new things were that he was encountering. There were no naturalists, metallurgists or clergy on board. Kirkpatrick Sale, *The Conquest of Paradise: Chrisopher Columbus and the Columbian Legacy*, (New York: Knopf, 1990), 11-13. The fact that there were no clergy on board flies in the face of the Columbus myth especially as it is imagined by Hollywood. Columbus in the

movies is accompanied by priests and sometimes friars carrying crosses as they hit the beach as he makes land on his first voyage of discovery.

[6] Wilford, 219.

[7] Wilford, 230. Military historians have made it clear that with the fall of Acre in 1292 any possibility of recapturing the Holy Land in a Crusade was at best a backwards looking delusion. This did not of course prevent dreamers from Dante to Columbus to today's Zionists from being gripped by the heroic fantasy of such a religious mission.

[8] Wilford, 231. In 1455 Pope Nicholas V empowered the king of Portugal to "invade, search out, capture, vanquish, and subdue all Saracens and pagans whatsoever, and other enemies of Christ wheresoever placed." The Portuguese took these instructions to sanction their raids on Muslims in North Africa and to legitimize slaving operations among the black "pagan" peoples along the West African coast.

[9] It must be remembered though that Columbus needed this single-mindedness to assail and get to the other side of the Atlantic Ocean, the Ocean Sea as it was then called, the largest body of water known at that time by Europeans. It took an American poet like Charles Olson to point out something as obvious as this. See Charles Olson, *Call Me Ishmael* (San Francisco: City Lights Books, 1947), 12.

[10] *Vespucci's Letters*, 45.

[11] See *Vespucci's Letters*.

[12] In particular see William Cronon, *Changes in the Land: Indians, Colonists, and the Ecology of New England* (New York: HarperCollins, 1983), and James Axtell, *The Invasion Within: The Contest of Cultures in Colonial North America* (New York: Oxford UP, 1985).

[13] Just to mention, for example, a major cultural launching pad, Shakespeare's monstrous and slavish character, Caliban, in *The Tempest*, reflects this view of how "America," the place, transforms and adversely effects a human. Caliban, because of his living on this island, becomes physically deformed, ugly, mentally weak, and morally deficient.

[14] This essay will try to address the subject from a different point of view—though it must be said that there can be no exclusively so-called "American" point of view or "Native American" point of view or "African-American" point of view or even "anti-European" point of view. The reason is because

"we" are all so mixed and homogenized that these ethnic or political distinctions are past the point of being true except as each individual imagines them.

[15] The great eleventh edition of *The Encyclopædia Britannica* says in reference to Buffon, "Of handsome person and noble presence, endowed with many of the external gifts of nature, and rejoicing in the social advantages of high rank and large possessions, he is mainly known by his published scientific writings. Without being a profound original investigator, he possessed the art of expressing his ideas in a clear and generally attractive form. His chief defects as a scientific writer are that he was given to excessive and hasty generalization, so that his hypotheses, however seemingly brilliant, are often destitute of any sufficient basis in observed facts," [unsigned article] "Buffon, George Louis Leclerc," *The Encyclopædia Britannica*, 11th ed., 4 (1911): 758.

Buffon was a member of the Academy of of Arts and Sciences of Dijon which awarded Rousseau first prize in the year 1750 for his essay. This essay led to the development of Rousseau's concept of the Noble Savage.

[16] Buffon's thesis was based on his idea that America's natural world suffered an arrested development due to excess humidity caused by its late emergence out of the waters of the Biblical flood. Wilford, 270-71.

[17] In *Philosophical Researches on the American*, published in Berlin in 1768, a Dutch writer, Cornelius de Pauw, declared "It is without doubt a terrible spectacle to see one half of the globe so disfavoured by nature that everything there is degenerate or monstrous." Like so many Europeans who have pronounced and written on America, from Peter Martyr to Montaigne to Rousseau to Buffon, De Pauw came to this conclusion having never once traveled there.

[18] For several centuries colonial Spanish women would return from New Spain to have their children born in Europe so that they would be European and not American. The Royal Spanish colonial administration reinforced this practice by setting up prejudicial inheritance and citizenship laws in their American colonies, favoring those colonials born in Europe over colonials unfortunate enough to be born in New Spain. Specifically all senior colonial administrators had to be born in Spain. Throughout the history of Spain's American colonies, these officials were sarcastically and perhaps enviously referred to by the *criollos* or American born Spaniards, as *peninsulares*, meaning having been born on the Iberian peninsula and in line for preferment in holding colonial offices. See *Americas Lost: 1492-1713 The First Encounter*, ed. Daniel Lévine, foreword Claude Lévi-Strauss, trans. John Fegusson and Michael Barry, (Paris: Bordas SA, 1992), 24.

Although such policies look odd today, it should not be forgotten that after Charles II was restored to the English throne, even British Americans were almost never appointed as the highest colonial officials, and British Americans had no representation in Britain's parliament. This was because, as colonials, they were eurocentrically viewed by the English aristocracy as, at best, suspect and inferior Englishmen.

The exception to this was the sugar island colonies in the British West Indies. In the eighteenth century the English Caribbean sugar plantations were so wealthy and powerful, they were allowed representation in Parliament. When North American colonial representatives, in their quest for representation, pointed this out to parliamentarians in London, it was consequently explained to them that, well of course, they did not need seats in the House of Commons as, of course, the sugar growers represented them!

The eighteenth century English ruling class believed and was fond of saying that their North American colonies were peopled by religious fanatics and criminals. English politicians at that time felt a colony populated by religious nuts and thieves that was costing more money than it was returning to England was certainly not deserving of any legislative representation. This ruling British attitude, along with corrupt royal officials and heavy taxation, led to the American Revolution and the founding of the United States.

[19] In *The Philosophical and Political History of Institutions and Commerce of the Two Indies* published in 1770 in Amsterdam, the French *philosophe* Abbé Guillaume-Thomas Raynal (1713-1796) wrote that Europeans who became "Americans" were "a new species of anomalous savages." This book was popular *until the middle of the nineteenth century*, and so not only is it doubtful that he was alone in this opinion of Europeans who had become Americans but also its popularity to such a late date probably has had an indirect effect on how Europeans view Americans today.

If we may cite the eleventh edition of *The Encyclopædia Britannica* once more (it is, after all, unsurpassed by later editions), it says of this work, "Diderot indeed is credited with a third of this work, which was characterized by Voltaire as *du réchauffé avec de la declamation.* The other chief collaborators were Pechméja, Holbach, Paulze, the farmer-general of taxes, the Abbé Martin, and Alexandre Deleyre. To this piecemeal method of composition, in which narrative alternated with tirades on political and social questions, was added the further disadvantage of the lack of exact information, which, owing to the dearth of documents, could only have been gained by personal investigation. ... The History went through many editions ... it was translated into the principal European languages ... Its introduction into France was forbidden in 1779; the book was burned by the public executioner, and an order was given for the arrest of the author". [unsigned article], "Raynal, Guillaume Thomas François," *The Encyclopædia Britannica*, 11th ed., 22 (1911): 936. It must be pointed out that the Royal French government hated this book and its author not because of its anti-Americanism but because it put forth inflammatory and revolutionary ideas.

[20] This has been expressed in writers as diverse as Walt Whitman and Ezra Pound, and from Henry James to Charles Olson. Especially see Pound's musings on the *periplum* in his epic *The Cantos* and Charles Olson's understanding of space as defining America in *Call me Ishmael*.

[21] This was the name of the pre-Columbian inhabitants of Hispaniola.

[22] *Americas Lost*, 22-23.

[23] See Olson, 11.

[24] Of course this was published in an American journal. See Kathleen Raine, "Revisioning the Sacred," *Alexandria* 1 (1991): 23. A few years ago in Switzerland, I met a Swiss who had just returned from the Yucatan. He said he had just spent three months looking at the remains of ancient Mayan culture. Although he claimed that he found the culture interesting, yet still he concluded that Europe and its art was far and away superior.

[25] A case in point is the American born and raised psychologist James Hillman (the retiring senior editor of this journal), who on returning to the United States after having lived in Europe for thirty years, said in his book, *Inter Views*, "America just isn't a psychological place. You have to be immersed in Europe to be psychological." A bit further in the book he continues with this prejudice by saying that American "personal closeness is an attempt to go deeper in a culture where there are no deep ideas, no structures of depth." This implies, if one knows how Hillman values depth, that America is indeed on the short end when compared to Europe's profundity. Of course at that time, he was not aware to what degree C. G. Jung was influenced by William James. A little later in the book he says in explaining why he was drawn to live in Paris and go to the Sorbonne in the 1940's, ". . . I was dying for intellectual life. It wasn't the university but to be intellectual. That was something an American doesn't know about. If you want to be intellectual, you are academic". James Hillman, *Inter Views*, 1983 (rpt. Woodstock, Conn.: Spring Publications, 1997), 93, 97, 98. Evidently Hillman had forgotten about North America's non-academic intellectual tradition which includes people like Ben Franklin, Thomas Jefferson, Edgar Allan Poe, Ralph Waldo Emerson, Nathaniel

Hawthorne, Herman Melville, Walt Whitman, William Carlos Williams, Wallace Stevens, Arthur Miller, Charles Olson, Edmund Wilson, and Robert Duncan. Hillman, it seems, had come to identify with the Eurocentric American expatriates of the modern era (i.e., T. S. Eliot, Henry Miller, Ernest Hemingway, Man Ray, Gertrude Stein and his friend, J. P. Donleavy) and European cafe *intellos*.

[26] Wilford, 3, 174.

[27] More graduate students study Early American Literature in English departments in the United States than any other area.

[28] Evidently this was how he was characterized by his Harvard students in the 30's. Tom Clark, *Charles Olson: The Allegory of a Poet's Life* (New York: Norton, 1991), 39-40.

[29] Perry Miller, *Errand into the Wilderness*, 1956 (rpt. New York: Harper & Row, 1964), vii, viii.

[30] Miller, *Errand*, 1.

[31] William Bradford, *Of Plymouth Plantation*, ed. Samuel Eliot Morison (New York: Knopf, 1952), xxiv.

[32] It was then lent to Judge Sewall and so to the Rev. Thomas Prince's library in the steeple of the Old South Church in Boston. It was stolen from there by British troops during the Revolution and ended up in the Bishop of London's library after the Revolution. It was not returned to Boston by the English until 1897.

[33] Bradford, 62.

[34] Bradford, 63.

AMERICAN EDUCATION: HORROR OF EXPERIENCE

GREG NIXON

W hat god does educational experience serve? Education in any country in any time or place serves the interests of the state. Why else would there be state-supported, state-mandated education? In this sense, one should be little surprised at the evolution of education in America. Evolving out of forms of parochial instruction on this continent, state-mandated education has always taken that fearful raw material—the individual soul—and striven mightily to make it forget its nature and to build an officially approved memorialization in its place based on the state's imperatives.

The first recognized state-mandated school on this continent was in fact legislated by New England Puritans in righteous indignation against the shadow side of natural impulse. "The Old Deluder Satan Act" (e.g.,Pulliam & Van Patten, 1995) was passed to ensure that individual families did not become lax in their exorcising of any potential demonic influences upon village youth.[1] The most feared result of imperfect parental vigilance, it seems, was idleness.

Greg Nixon is a professor of the philosophy of education in the New York State University system.

In such idleness, thoughts may wander, imagination may awaken, and who knows what visitations may occur?

The attitude had gone full circle from that of Arcadian Hellas when the leisurely shepherd might anticipate all sorts of imaginal visitations, including that trickster of the woods, Satan's inspiration, Pan. Early in America, however, gods were excluded. Serving God the Father was work, not divine encounter. Visitation—transformation—was outlawed.

In spite of the continuous hue and cry for educational reform ever since then, in the broadest sense little has changed. Public education in these United States still means, simply, socialization, just as the Supreme Court expects it should (Whitson, 1991). Schools continue to exist for the sake of narrowing the road to *success*: measurement, placement, elimination of the many along the way and election of the chosen few who have become most successfully systematized. Schools are themselves systems which flow into other systems, economic and political. When schools work, the individual identifies her experience with that of the social monopoly, allowing its desires and fears to become her desires and fears. In a subtle life-term form of self-sacrifice, the person becomes a citizen whose moods reflect the rise and fall of the GDP or other economic indicators of success. Is it any wonder that schooling has been rejected by much of American youth?[2]

But this is not going to be a discourse on the need for further reform—reforms which will (according to the reformer) at last usher in the Golden Age of both American education and, as a consequence, American society. Reforms of all sorts have been attempted and (as is my job to note) are still being attempted. Voices from the Right call for a privatized school voucher system and from the Left for decentralized community-run schools. Both seem to feel the tyranny of the center. Both margins (and other margins not included here) feel that their versions of the human experience—and the human imperative for experience—are being left out of the mandatory mass education of American children. They see instrumental indoctrination and the destruction of "true" values, whether those are values of egalitarian community (Left) or those of a chosen elect (Right). And they are not wrong. For in the midst of this ongoing turmoil for reform is the pervasive intuition of the meaninglessness of the entire educational project.[3]

Even today what I recall most about my elementary schooling is the excitement of recess or the burst of energy when we were released at the end of the school day. For an energetic child to sit long hours day after day in those stupid rows of desks is as excruciatingly *boring* as it is without meaning.

Why is it meaningless? Because, no matter how sugar-coated the pill has become—no matter how many research projects have been undertaken to make it more palatable—schooling still asks people to give up the potential of their individual souls for the sake of the "greater good" of the collective. To some extent, such a sacrifice must be made for societies to exist. But in our mass society, the denial of experience in our dream of planned education has never been more blatant or destructive because of its very mass. Youthful yearnings usually have no specific content and so are quite amenable to being channeled into public streams. Public streams, however, leave little opportunity for the exploration of one's secret tributaries or direct encounters with the underground currents of the soul's reality. The call for change or reform is a call for more assured production—not for changes in the intensity of individual experience.

The meaninglessness of public education is made especially apparent by contrasting it with its garish carnival twin: popular culture. Both systems create values and goals and, in the original Latin sense of drawing forth the soul,[4] both systems educate. Public schooling attempts to make clear its direction and offers images of economic security and social respect. Popular culture makes nothing clear and offers instead images of an endless circus of personal experience—both riotous and serene, benign and deadly. In this contrast we see how the yearning soul has found its objects of allure elsewhere than in the sterile corridors of the nation's schools. Popular culture is built of layers of exciting simulacra, whispers from the dark—the Old Deluder's dream. "But that is not the purpose of schooling," I can hear the voices of my colleagues speaking with aggravated patience. "The institutions of education are supposed to prepare children for a productive life in society."

This brings up the whole question of the kind of society we envision—which asks ultimately about the relation between soul and world as T. S. Eliot stated in 1932:

> Education is a subject which cannot be discussed in a void: our questions raise other questions, social, economic, financial, political. And the bearings are on more ultimate problems even than these: to know what we want in education we must know what we want in general; we must derive our theory of education from our philosophy of life. The problem turns out to be a religious problem. (171)

Yet though Eliot brought the question back to its origin among the gods, his sort of intellectual quandary is not the fundament that raw, transformational experience provides. All knowing must begin with a knower who is ready to learn, and the old adage, experience is the best teacher, goes far deeper than first meets the eye. There is the image of learning through accumulation, the student as empty vessel to be filled, the traditional teaching of rote memory. (Today the preferred image is that of the central processing unit in the computer which stores input in data storage banks, does calculations, and provides output upon the appropriate keyboard request from an outside programmer.) In contrast is the image of experience in this world which heads out, like a knight errant, uncertain of its destination. In the former case, input knowledge overwhelms any chance for personal encounter. In the latter case, the experience precedes the knowledge.

The philosopher who was most concerned with experience and education in America was John Dewey. In 1938, Dewey noted the cascade effect of experience which "modifies the one who acts and undergoes, while this modification affects, whether we wish it or not, the quality of subsequent experiences" (35). In this implication of the past in the present, one can see how experience allows for the possibility of knowing. Yet to what sort of experiencing was Dewey referring? At this time he was backing away from some of the extremes of the Progressive Education movement and clearly identified valuable experience with experience guided toward known ends. He wrote that experience "can be judged only on the ground of what it moves toward and into," and that "all human experience is ultimately social" (38). Dewey understood such valuable experience as referring to experience in problem solving, and the best way to approach problem solving was through the scientific method. Again, the image is one of mental experience and the accumulation of useful experience. Aside from the physical experience of athletics and activity in the arts, experience in schools has continued to be understood as mental or abstract. And even sports and theatre are supposed to have clear social benefits.

My true education in life arose mainly from encounters in violence and love. Only later, after my undergraduate degree, did I find my own intellectual path. A journey of understanding had become necessary to integrate the life altering experiences of youth. And this is what I am driving at: experience, to be worthy of its name, is exactly that, life altering. It is transformative. It leads to a metamorphosis in the soul of the life-traveller, even when the end of such a metamorphosis is unknown. Such journeys into experience are often terrifying because they are essentially journeys into the unknown. This is why transformative experience as I am portraying it is different from the conversion experience (in which the ends are known in advance). Transformative experience may take place on other levels than the abstractions of the mind—such as the emotions, the aesthetic sense, intuition, the "primal eye," or even in the body. It may have no social purpose whatsoever, and whether its nature is "ultimately social" or not is a moot point. It is this experience which was so fearful to the Puritans and remains a horror to the minds of educators and the "general public" today.

It should be noted that though schooling remains horrified at the prospects of transgressive imagination or actual life-altering experiences, this is not necessarily the perspective of those who think about what schooling ought to be. Many have called for the return of myth and story into the curricula of the land. James Hillman has repeatedly stated that the old myths need to be known so we can comprehend the mythic in our own life. In curriculum theory, Kieran Egan (1990, 1992) has called for a life of the romantic imagination in schools, especially in those crucial years of middle school when life's possibilities are explored through flights of fancy.

In the sixties and seventies, the voices of James B. Macdonald and Dwayne Huebner were among many which called for the creation of "meaning" in schools by speaking openly about elements of spirituality. More recently, Huebner has returned to the field, specifically pinpointing the scientific language of curriculum as displacing spirituality and the imagination. He asks, "How can one talk about education, specifically, curriculum, and also talk about the spiritual? We have forgotten or suppressed that imagination is a foundation of our givens" (1993, 1).

At this point, he sounds like Hillman who continually restates his understanding of the mythic imagination as the fundamental reality. It is in this light that Hillman calls for *Healing Fictions* (1983), recognizing the need for fictional story telling over the need for the factual data in construction of our life stories. Strangely, however, Hillman does not consider such a healing process for education: "Which stories need to be told? Here I am orthodox, holding for the old, the traditional, the ones of our own culture: Greek, Roman, Celtic, and Nordic myths; the Bible; legends and folk tales" (1979a, 45). Though this statement is nearly twenty years old, it remains at least dubious that simply learning traditional monocultural stories provides much hope for transformation.

William F. Pinar and others have suggested that the stories which need to be told, deconstructed, and retold again are those of our lives. By opening up the enclosure habitual language has built around our experience—by, in essence, mythmaking—we may open ourselves to experience beyond the clutter of language. Our life stories are the "healing fictions" which may bring us in touch with the extra-social divinities of the heart. "It is awareness that there is a 'beyond' to our knowledge that is the beginning of the theological," Pinar has written (Pinar et al., 1995, 861). How far one dare follow this "beyond" into unknown realms of experience in the contexts of education remains an unanswerable question at present. Truly raw experience tends to draw the experiencer out of (or before) society, and since education is social, it is difficult to imagine the sort of education which could provide the nexus for the experience of archetypal forces.

This precisely seems to have been among the purposes of ritual and initiation. Experience of the unknown, however, is less Van Gennep's (1960) *Rites of Passage* into social acceptance than Joseph Campbell's (1949) journey of the hero (though Campbell's hero is portrayed as always returning to society, like a bodhisattva, bringing a "boon"). Though memorialized and commemorated from the reports of previous revelations, this "unknown" can only be known in itself, without any of the detritus of social convention for the first time for each individual who brings his experience into it. Signposts for such experience were once among the roles of myth. Myth can open the portals for individual journeys into meaning (though, misused, myth can just as easily close them).

Campbell's often cited four functions of a mythology may be relevant here and can be summarized thus. The first is the cosmic or what I would call the archetypal: to reconcile individual consciousness to the sea of the unknown—the *mysterium tremendum*—on which it rests. The second is the cosmological or religious: to create an image of the great mystery meaningful to the times so it may communicate "from heart to heart by way of the brain." The third is the social: to justify the moral order and customs of society (presumably into which the youth are to be socialized). Fourth is the psychological or developmental: to guide the individual through the stages of life according to the demands of society, religion, the universe at large, and the great unknown (Campbell, 1968, 4-6).

It is not my purpose to recommend that our education take up all the functions of a mythology, but since Campbell's functions are so all encompassing, it may behoove us to see just how our public institutions of "leading or drawing forth" are guiding the individual through the sound and fury of a lifetime. Clearly, we can put function number one by the wayside. The most officially sanctioned source of revelation in our era is science, and neither physics nor biology nor chemistry nor astronomy have given us any reason to feel certain a *mysterium tremendum* even exists or is possible.[5] Schooling is not about mysteries or feelings of a "we" but about "getting down to the business of learning." Of what use is a "we?"

The same applies to Campbell's function number two. Since Thomas Jefferson made sure that church and state evolved as separate entities, it has been understood that there were to be no messages leaping "from heart to heart by way of the brain" in our schools. Schools are welcome to teach objectively about religions or myths, meaning their practices, beliefs, and historical consequence. But the phenomenology of religious experience is avoided—at least until the student is far enough along to be well filtered by layers of rational skepticism.

So what does that leave the institutions of education with which to open the potential for meaningful experience? Looking at the history of education in America, it seems evident that schools have emerged solely from mythic function number three and basically continue to serve it. They are the agents of socialization and enforcement of the moral order. In our world we have the potent images of the factory and the corporate ladder to add to our sense of efficient guidance and quality control. Since their inception during the nineteenth century era of mass immigration (with nominal sidetracks for Dewey and progressive education, and later, Rogerian humanistic education), public "common" schools have basically met the needs of a society perceived as being in a state of mobilization against external forces of disintegration, corruption from within (from unions to gangs), or even the danger of falling behind other nations in terms of productivity or test scores. In this situation, it has been understood that it is the "duty" of schools to turn out citizens who will be loyal, industrious, and obedient, i.e., socialized into the capitalistic moral order. The only carrot held before such student raw material is that of employment and ownership of a supply of consumer goods. With such experientially meaningless motivation, it is no shock that increasing numbers of students opt out for one of the versions of the futureless cool of carnival culture.

Schools should be ideal places to institutionalize Campbell's mythic function number four, that of being a guide through the stages of life—if only we could figure out what these stages are. Here we again see the assumptions of the sociological function spilling over to contain theorizing about developmental transformation. The big name in stage theory remains Jean Piaget, but his highest stage of development—that of formal operations or abstract reasoning—is attained by the age of eleven or twelve. That leaves a whole lifetime ahead in which the individual can apply his or her abstract reasoning to the betterment of society without expecting any new *gestalts* at all. Other stage theorists, such as the textbook neo-Freudian Erik Erikson, are more liberal in the breadth of time periods during which transformation is possible, but even they do not conceive anything as abrupt as the transformation absorbed during an actual rite of passage.

C. G. Jung, whom some see as a developmental theorist because of his work on typologies, envisioned a major alteration of worldview and life experience somewhere around midlife which he called individuation, but he seems to have largely felt such to be a phenomenon of nature which an individual must encounter on one's own (or with a good analyst). His disciple and sometimes rival, Erich Neumann (1954), went much further in his bold and compelling fantasies of stages of conscious development as evidenced in myth. In the examples of Jung and Neumann, what may be called a spiritual or transcendent dimension is implied as the aim of inner metamorphosis. "Spiritual," however, remains a loaded word in our era of fundamentalist retrenchment, and "transcendent" smacks of gurus or the psychedelic era.

A less elevated image may be suggested by Maurice Merleau-Ponty's path to transcendence, a path not forward but one which spirals back into itself, unpredictably: "If being is to unveil itself, it will be in the face of a transcendence and not an intentionality; it will be brute being caught in the shifting sands, a being that reverts to itself: it will be the sensible hollowing itself out" (1968, 210). This vision seems to suggest a return to the source of memory rather than an epiphany of the Holy. In Mircea Eliade's sense such transcendence often involved the abolishment of time through its return to mythic origins. This path was taken in orgiastic rituals by archaic groups according to Eliade (1959), though the experience of immersion in the *illud tempus* and the consequent loss of identity must have been experienced always as "the first time" since it was felt to be out of time entirely (without befores).

Such "orgiastic" experience seems to take us to the opposite pole from spirituality. Instead of transcendence, transformation, or trans-anything, it suggests the experience of the senses and the impulsive nature of intoxication. If education in America fears the spiritual or transcendent, it is horrified at the possibility of altered states of consciousness. This may go right back to the Puritans and their obsession with cleansing the world of impulse and imagination. If the Old Deluder gets into the mind, he may be revealed as Nature unleashed—perhaps Pan—out to lead the children back to the Garden of the Senses. Yet again the delusion could turn out to be golden Aphrodite, always sure to stiffen the waywardness of Puritan youths. Or the Old Deluder may be revealed as the paragon of intoxicated madness himself—Dionysos—demonic /daimonic indeed.[6]

Norman O. Brown (1959, 1966), that avenger of the instincts, has declared all humankind to be heading toward mass extinction through the strangulation of repressive self-control unless we awaken to ecstasy and evolve Dionysian egos. Zorba the Greek felt the same.[7] I am not sure how practical such a notion is for the schools of this, the most philo-technical driven society the world has ever seen, but the temptations for an experience starved populace are real.[8] Are we to take Nietzsche's suggestion of the Apollonian / Dionysian dichotomy and conclude that the aridity of the educational establishment is due to its being too deeply enlightened by the sphere of bright Apollo? Is our learning too culti-vated, too intellectual, too harmonious? If this is the case, simply to rush blindly into such Dionysian experience as is promised by popular culture is not likely to balance things out. As Ginette Paris has written, "If any given culture receives only Apollonian sunshine, it dries up and dies; conversely, if it receives too much Dionysian moisture, it rots and becomes crazy. A hyper-technologized, hyper-rationalized society is as crazy, in a way, as is an anti-intellectual rock 'n roll subculture. We need both Dionysos and Apollo" (1990).

But surely we have them both in the split between the popular culture of personal experience and the educational system of cultivated intellect. Although the former may be the case, the latter is no longer true. Our education system, though often dry, rarely attains Apollonic status. In traditional education it was felt to be true that a good education made one cultivated and more in touch with the revealed truths of bygone ages; that the more learning one absorbed, the nearer one was to the eternal. "I am the eye with which the Universe / Beholds itself, and knows it is divine," the poet Shelley has Apollo declare.

Since American pragmatism swept the land clear of such foolish pretensions as culture for its own sake, the purpose of education has been as a procurer for industry and technology. After traditional education was declared inadequate, progressive education carried the torch onward but in two sharply divided directions. As indicated, Dewey looked to a child-centered education in which the student could be gradually lured into democratic participation. On the other hand, taking its cue from F. W. Taylor's scientific management practices in industry and the measurement-placement tactics of E. L. Thorndike and Charles Eliot, the other direction saw education as an instrument of social efficiency which would provide workers for the progress of the nation as an industrial power (e.g., see Tozer, Violas, & Senese, 1995). With the advent of behaviorism and, since the 80s, the demand for basics, accountability, and national standardization, education today pays scant attention to the narratives of culture. It has instead become the eager supplier for the grand march of civilization.

James Hillman has expressed doubt that there are gods or "invisibles" in such a civilization as a whole. He too has scorned the loss of experiential depth in contemporary life:

> Civilization looks ahead, culture looks back. Civilization is histori-cal record; culture a mythic enterprise. . . . Culture. . .looks backwards and reaches back as a nostalgia for invisibilities, to make them present and to found human life upon them. The cultural enterprise attempts to peel, flail, excite individual sensitivity so that it can again—notice the "again"—be in touch with these invisibles and orient life by their compass. (1986, 17)

Culture, then, is the Apollonian, the cultivated. The release of untamed impulse is Dionysian. Neither one can be found to any extent in today's schools. Education, like a smoothly functioning computerized assembly line, dreams of the perfection of the machine (no matter how cliché, cute, or unlikely that sounds). The voices calling for experience or cultivation are ridiculed. Denied experience, there is only one conclusion possible: American education is godless indeed. It is both what the Puritans most feared and most desired.

The institution of education—and all institutions—seems to fit only within the orbit of the senex archetype. Despite the suggestion of a Saturn / Kronos deification of the senex archetype, it seems more likely that the senex is an aspect of all archetypes. It is the ordered identity into which the archetype evolves: the institutionalized ego. For Hillman, "the senex archetype...is given from the beginning as a potential of order, meaning, and teleological fulfillment—and death—within all the psyche and all its parts....It is the death that comes through perfectionand order" (1979b, 18). In this sense, it can be seen that the senex triumphs whenever schools become productive, successful, and obliterate any potential for the transformative visitations of puer sensibilities: "As principle of coagulation and of geometrical order, [senex] dries and orders, 'builds cities' and 'mints money,' makes solid and square and profitable, overcoming the dissolving wetness of soulful emotionality" (19). The American institution is itself the senex aspect of all the psyche's aspirations and, as such, its unconscious effloresces darkly.

The horror of experience has reached such extremes that even the proponents of rational balance come off sounding like the highly irrational Puritans of old. It has reached the extent where any mention of uncondoned individual experience— whether transcendent, emotional, or intoxicated—receives a blanket condemnation. The whole terror implied by the generic term "drugs" is a metaphor for what the Puritan rationalists consider to be unspeakable, even unthinkable: unplanned, unguided experience.

We have now reached the point where an attorney-general can lose her position for merely suggesting that decriminalization of drugs might be investigated,[9] where one middle school girl can be suspended for sharing Midol tablets and another for sharing cough drops with zinc and yet another for having ibuprofen in her locker. The selling of compressed nitrous oxide capsules can be declared illegal even in Le Vieux Carré in New Orleans (despite no suggestion of side affects or after affects in such small doses). The term "drugs" has apparently crossed the illegal /legal boundary to now include everything up to and often including vitamin pills. Can there be a more blatant sign of the fear of experience? What is behind this—the fear of altering our objective perception of God's perfectly predictable little puppet, *H. Sapiens*—or fear that individuals may see through the façade of living only for the reified self of the collective?

I am not suggesting school reforms; the reforms of which I dream would leave the school system unrecognizable. Nor am I suggesting that we include experimental drugs as part of the curriculum. What I am doing is indulging in some archetypal blues. Where is the quaking awe of Campbell's function number one? Where is the "communion" of function number two? Though I recognize that the dropping of the wall of separation between religion and schooling would be insane in this time period of continued religious zealotry, I still lament that experience which may be understood as transcendent (or even spiritual) is considered anathema. With even more unease, I watch the good, successful students march forward, ignoring or resisting the drawing power of desire that beckons from the depths of soul.

I lament that the drama students I once taught felt the necessity of resisting the full intoxication of their art because they did not know where it would take them. Some actually reported that I was leading them into hypnotic trances and others that the improvisation made them feel the devil was being conjured. The Old Deluder remains present still but now has himself become an institutionalized senex instilling in the "good children" the wish to make a difference and reform society—but also to convince them of the ghastly horror of the ecstatic possession found in breakthrough experiences. I lament the watchful veiled eyes, ever on the lookout for signs of untoward emotion, or imagination taking wing, or any invisibilities which may be loitering in the vicinity of school.

In short, the American school of which I dream would either be much smaller—openly a training school for future employees—dropping the charade that life in schools is a portrayal of the way real life ought to be lived. Or the American school would have to leave its classrooms and buildings and become much larger, merging with its archrival—popular culture—and seeking out the range of potential experience wherever it may be found even if the quest be recklessly called "religious" or "ecstatic." Only in this way can a space be opened for the possibility of intrinsic meaning to reveal itself or be created. Only then would metamorphic experience become the inspiration—the teacher—of cultural life, rather than the evil twin whose return is always dreaded.

Notes

[1] The Act was passed in Massachusetts in 1647. It required townships of over fifty families to have a reading and writing tutor, and townships of over one hundred families to maintain a strict grammar school.

[2] This includes youth still in school. Thomas Toch states, "By one estimate as many as two-thirds of the nation's public secondary students are 'disengaged' from their studies" (1991, 235).

[3] According to Toch (1991), the sense of meaninglessness experienced by both students and teachers is more than intuition. His surveys cite it as the primary malaise of public schooling.

[4] Latin: *educere*: to lead or draw forth.

[5] Though there is plenty of fine scientific writing from "out there," check the New Age section of your bookstore.

[6] "A god who is mad! A god, part of whose nature it is to be insane! What did they experience or see—these people on whom the horror of this concept must have forced itself?" (Otto, 1965, 136).

[7] "A man needs a little madness, or else he dare never cut the rope and be free!" (Zorba the Greek via Nikos Kazantzakis, 1953)

[8] "We long for a holiday from our frontal lobes, a Dionysiac fiesta of sense and impulse" (Sacks, 1995, 64).

[9] This persists despite well-documented research by Ronald K. Siegel (1989) showing that most sentient creatures seek altered states or intoxication on

occasion. Still, there are no research programs planned to develop a safe, nonaddictive disinhibitor or stimulant. Research is underway to find pain suppressants that avoid the undesired (by doctors!) side effect of euphoria. All research on LSD and other psychedelics has been illegal since the late 60s in spite of protests by experts in the field who state that psychedelics may have potentially healing benefits in such areas as addiction therapy and mental illness. And despite the fact that a majority of Americans use some sort of "drug" for pleasure.

References

Brown, Norman O. *Life Against Death*. Wesleyan, Conn.: Wesleyan UP, 1959.

_____. *Love's Body*. Berkley, Calif.: University of California Press, 1966.

Campbell, Joseph. *The Hero of a Thousand Faces*. Princeton: Bollingen Foundation, Princeton UP, 1949.

_____. *The Masks of God: Creative Mythology*. New York: Viking, 1968.

Dewey, John. *Experience and Education*. Kappa Delta Pi (rpt. Collier Macmillan), 1938.

Egan, Kieran. *Romantic Understanding: The Development of Rationality and Imagination, Ages 8-15*. London: Routledge, 1990.

_____. *Imagination in Teaching and Learning*. Chicago: University of Chicago Press, 1992.

Eliade, Mircea. *The Sacred and the Profane*. Tr. W. R. Trask. New York: Harcourt, Brace, Jovanovich, 1959.

Eliot, T. S. "Modern Education and the Classics." 1932. Rpt. in *Essays: Ancient and Modern*. London: Faber & Faber, 1936.

Hillman, James. "A note on story." *Parabola*, IV, 1979a, 43-46.

_____. "Senex and Puer." *Puer Papers*. Irving, Tex.: Spring Publications, 1979b. Original 1967.

_____. *Healing Fictions*. Dallas: Spring Publications, 1983.

_____. "On Culture and Chronic Disorder." *Stirrings of Culture: Essays from the Dallas Institute*. Eds. Robert Sardello and Gail Thomas. Dallas: Dallas Institute Publications, 1986.

Huebner, D. *Education and Spirituality*. New Haven, Conn: Yale University, The Divinity School, unpublished manuscript. (Presented to the Seminar on Spirituality and Curriculum, November 20, 1993, Loyala University, New Orleans, Louisiana.)

Kazantzakis, Nikos, *Zorba the Greek*. Tr. C. Wildman. New York: Simon & Shuster.

Merleau-Ponty, Maurice. *The Visible and the Invisible*. Tr. Alphonso Lingis. Evanston, Ill.: Northwestern UP, 1968.

Neumann, Erich. *The Origins and History of Consciousness*. Bollingen Foundation/Princeton UP, 1954.

Otto, Walter. *Dionysos: Myth and Cult*. Indiana UP. Original in German, 1933. Spring Publications reprint, 1989.

Paris, Ginette. *Pagan Grace: Dionysos, Hermes, and Goddess Memory in Daily Life*. Tr. Johanna Mott. Dallas: Spring Publications, 1990.

Pinar, W. F., W. M. Reynolds, P. Slattery, P. M. Taubman. *Understanding Curriculum*. New York: Peter Lang, 1995.

Pulliam, J. D. and J. Van Patten. *History of Education in America* (6th ed.). New York: Prentice-Hall/Simon & Shuster, 1995.

Sacks, Oliver. *An Anthropologist on Mars*. New York: Alfred A. Knopf, 1995.

Shelley, P. B. "Song of Apollo." *Selected Poems*. New York: Gramercy Books, 1994. Originally published in the early 1800s.

Siegel, R. K. *Intoxication*. New York: E. P. Dutton, 1989.

Toch, T. *In the Name of Excellence: The Struggle to Reform the Nation's Schools, Why It's Failing, and What Should Be Done*. London: Oxford UP, 1991.

Tozer, S. E., P. C. Violas, and G. B. Senese. *School and Society* (2nd Ed.). New York: McGraw-Hill, 1995.

Van Gennep, A. *The Rites of Passage*. Chicago: University of Chicago Press, 1960.

Whitson, J. A. *Constitution and Curriculum*. London: Falmer Press, 1991.

THE VIETNAM WAR
AND THE AMERICAN SHADOW

EDWARD TICK

I. The Mythic Arena of War

When bombs fall and bullets fly, when guns rattle, when men charge and scream and grapple, when forests and mountains burn, when the earth fragments beneath or around us, surely we are in a merciless arena; an arena of extremes. During battle, the heart beats too hard. Adrenaline pumps fast. Muscles, bones, and mind strain beyond capacity and still perform. Thoughts and feelings fly by as quickly as bullets and disappear unrecognized. Sensations bombard far too quickly to be processed.

And then it stops. Suddenly, though the system is still in overdrive, all is still. The world returns to its quietude. We try to awaken from the trance-like experience. We look around. Where there was a forest or a village, we see fire and devastation. People, perhaps just body parts, are scattered at our feet. We shake our heads, remember our humanity, look for our friends. But some of them, with whom we were just talking, are groaning in pain. Some just lie at our feet and will never respond to us again. The world has returned to

Edward Tick is a psychotherapist and writer who lives in Albany, New York. He specializes in treating veterans who suffer from Post-traumatic Stress Disorder.

us, but suddenly it is different forever. We have helped make it so. We do not know exactly how or why, but we too are different forever.

Nor do we have the time to figure out who or what we have become. The waiting and watching start in again. Though we are still frightened, days may pass with nothing to do but the most routine of tasks. We become bored. Our boredom too reaches an extreme and can be worse than battle. We long to break the tedium that has no other outlet but through the gun which we have been trained to shoot, and at these other human beings we have been taught to call "enemy." Finally we crave battle.

Under such distress, we are in an arena comprised of the most elemental conditions. Under such conditions some of us may behave with great courage. Under these same conditions, and with the dictum "kill or be killed" ruling our survival, some of us may also display the greatest cruelty or cowardice.

War tears open and destroys ordinary categories of existence. It blasts the participant with experiences of supernatural intensity, as if each participant were in a mythic dimension, full of forces of cosmic power, where only such ultimates as life and death, and getting through the day, and keeping your socks dry and your neighbor alive, matter. As the World War II correspondent Ernie Pyle wrote from the front lines, "War makes strange giant creatures out of us little routine men who inhabit the earth."[1] War is inherently a mythic arena.

What do war and its conditions do to our archetypal life? The soul's container and patterns are shattered. As James Hillman writes, "Some accidents swamp the boat, bust the form. For example, 'shell shock,' as post-traumatic stress disorder was called during the First World War..."[2] Homer tells us that during the Trojan War, Aphrodite was wounded by Diomedes and fled to Olympus for safety. In the same way during modern warfare, the soul itself is wounded by savagery and tries to flee its connections with this world.

War breaks open a society's forms as well, cracking our social containers so that the cultural shadow leaks out, revealing both the best and the worst in a culture and society as well as in its participants. "War is sweet to those who have not tried it," Pindar sang. "The experienced man is frightened at the heart to see it advancing."[3] As a willful activity chosen by a society, we civilized people believe that war is, or ought to be, the last resort; a final strategy used only under extreme and threatening conditions when all other options have failed.

Clearly, however, war is rarely such a last resort. It was used regularly and ritually, with significant containment and casualties kept to a minimum, in most traditional cultures. But in the history of mass civilizations, it appears regularly, usually with more patriotic exuberance than fright at its advance, certainly with far more destruction and death in its wake. War is an activity used more often and handily than we would wish.

Intimately tied to the human shadow, war reveals a great deal about a particular society's shadow. War invites all that is primitive, suppressed, denied, rationalized, or disguised in a particular culture to rush out unrestrained and display itself in all its savagery on that part of the globe chosen to temporarily serve as its arena. It is as if, during warfare, the tag-team of spirit and shadow of an entire culture pits itself in the arena against the tag-team of the opposing culture. To examine war from an archetypal perspective may thus help us see a culture's values as its entire moral and spiritual life swings its club.

No American war in living memory has been more controversial than the Vietnam War. We can turn to Vietnam veterans to examine our behavior as a culture-at-war. On both the personal and cultural levels, the Vietnam War reveals archetypal dimensions that America did not and still does not want to see.

II. The Vietnam War: Loss of Innocence and Shattering of Belief

While maintaining a private psychotherapy practice since 1976, I have specialized in the treatment of Vietnam and other war veterans, many of whom suffer Post-traumatic Stress Disorder. I also have directed a Veterans Treatment Program in New York State. While we cannot say that all Vietnam veterans suffer post-traumatic stress disorder, it is well established in the veterans' treatment field that "the vast majority of Vietnam-era veterans have had a much more problematic readjustment to civilian life than did their World War II and Korean War counterparts."[4] It is also understood that symptoms of post-traumatic stress disorder "are experienced by all Vietnam combat veterans to varying degrees."[5] Those veterans who are diagnosed are the ones likely to experience a majority of the disorder's symptoms in a chronic, debilitating manner.

Approximately 2.8 million individuals served in southeast Asia, one million seeing combat, with an average age of nineteen. As early as 1978, a half million of these had been diagnosed as having post-traumatic stress disorder,[6] "affecting not only the veteran but countless millions of persons who are in contact with them."[7] Not every veteran returned home with significant problems or has stress disorder. Yet the number of diagnosed cases has risen steadily over the last twenty years. Today, men and women in their forties, fifties, and sixties may still find their lives interrupted by that war's aftermath and seek treatment. These individuals, whose symptoms are trying to speak, enable us to examine the archetypal dimensions of the Vietnam War.

In nineteen years of treating Army, Navy, and Marine combat and non-combat veterans for the psychological aftermath of the Vietnam War, I have not treated a single veteran who feels, in retrospect, that that war or their service in it was correct, moral, justified, or honorable.

As a culture we have heard the pain and complaints of Vietnam veterans since they began returning from southeast Asia. Alienation, nightmares, flashbacks, violent behavior, drug and alcohol abuse, intimacy and employment problems, throwing medals at the Pentagon, refusing to vote or pay taxes, all began even before the war was over. Robert Jay Lifton's seminal psycho-historical work on veterans' suffering, *Home From the War*,[8] appeared as the bombs were still falling.

During the war the youth of this country, the generation being asked to fight in Vietnam, was in terrible pain. The veterans were letting us know their pain as soon as they returned. The massive protests, demonstrations, and actions staged at home against the war indicated overwhelming generational pain and doubt. Not to have adequately addressed the pain of our veterans either during the war or since, no matter what one's opinion on the correctness of the war, amounted to denial of the most overwhelming degree. One tank corps veteran said to me, "The main lesson I learned in Vietnam is that Denial is the name of the all-American disease."

What is being denied? That our youth, our families, our own, and an entire foreign nation were in pain. That we cannot participate in warfare without causing pain to ourselves and others. That war is utterly frightening and terrible. That America's prevailing cultural mythology of patriotism, super-heroism, geopolitical war of good against evil was terribly wrong and misleading in its depiction of war, its human consequences, and our true intentions. That in modern times warfare has become especially brutal because it is practiced with advanced technology devastating in its impact. That in modern times we do not practice war with the rituals and restraint that aid the participant in survival and recovery. That nobody can participate in modern warfare and emerge psychologically unscathed. That the pain of war does not go away when the bullets stop flying. That, as one jungle combat survivor wrote, "What you do, you become."[9] What one does in one moment under the most extreme conditions will define and shape that life forever. War teaches all these existential verities.

And all these are denied by American culture. As a culture we claim innocence, as though we Americans were above, or immune from, such unavoidable truths. We believe and behave as if we are doing God's work when we destroy other peoples and cultures. We transplanted ourselves from Europe and took this continent from its original inhabitants by force and within the protective context of a God-blessed mythology. As a nation we have been repeating our birth drama in like manner ever since. We Americans try to conquer other peoples and land "for their own good," or for our manifest destiny, because "we're number one," because we know and do better than other people, because it is our sacred task to slay an evil demon incarnate in the foreign other. And we seem to have had the special blessing-curse of having our "God-blessed-good-guy-at-war-to-stop-evil" mythology upheld and proven to us in World War II.

The Vietnam War was conducted within this mythological context. Many young soldiers who went to war, and Americans at home, believed we were doing the right thing in fighting the spread of the evil demon of Communism. The reports of atrocities in Vietnam, the failure of our political and military aims over so long a span of time, the pain, anger, and dysfunctionality of returning veterans did not teach us to shed our innocence and admit our darkness. The most devastating lesson to many of our veterans was the discovery that we as a nation and they as our agents were not the good cavalry saving the helpless settlers from savages or blessed crusaders slaying the black pajama-ed invaders from the Evil Empire. Rather they discovered that those we were trying to save saw us as the savage enemy needing to be stopped by their own painful, heroic sacrifices. This discovery shocked the archetypal foundation on which their psychology of goodness and innocence was based:

> I laid my gun across my legs and, while the Vietnamese family stared at me without daring to move, I stared out the door of their hut. That doorway was like a picture frame on the world... like I was staring out through God's eyes, looking down at Vietnam and all we were doing. I watched from this great distance... as... the men I fought with, the good guys, yelled like idiots and pushed these little people around.... I watched my buddies walk over to the hut right across from me... and torch it.... I looked at the family cowering in fear by my side. I looked across the way at my friend, the good guy, and another terrified mamasan....the flames... destroy[ing] her home.
>
> Suddenly I knew.... Something woke up in me. Good and evil. Honor and dishonor. Right and wrong. These had been automatic concepts... but at that moment... they were real, living things. You earned them by torturing yourself with questions until you really knew what was right and good and honorable, not because someone told you, but because you saw....
>
> I watched my buddies burn another hut, then another.... They weren't gooks, for God's sake!... They were a helpless mother and her terrified little children! After six months in the bush I saw them for the first time... They weren't evil. They weren't the enemies. They weren't the bad guys. We were!...

Everything was turned around. I swear, I knew who the bad guys were and I wanted to raise my M-16 and blast away at these crazy marauding Americans who were wasting this helpless village. Now I had a soul and I wanted to save it and these people by doing the right thing and defending them, even if it cost me my life....

I just walked off in a stupor while they... torched the hut. My hut with my family in it. Where I found my soul. Where I figured out the truth. I was in a daze for a long time. Then I went numb for the rest of my tour.... At the very moment I found my soul, at the very moment it woke up and I could see the truth for the first time in my life, at that very second when I knew we were evil, it fled, I lost it.[10]

A cloud of despair and a moral stain settled over America as a result of our behavior in Vietnam. It is as though the tens of thousands of veterans in chronic anguish are, collectively, the most apparent symptoms of our national soul-sickness regarding the Vietnam War. Though in distress, America still did not address the archetypal dimensions of the problem. Rather, as President Bush and military leaders indicated at the time, the Gulf War was staged, in large part, to overcome our Vietnam syndrome. George Bush confided to his diaries much the same thought that he declared in public—he wanted a decisive outcome to "finally kick in totally the Vietnam syndrome."[11] The public, political belief was that our national sickness of soul concerning the Vietnam War stemmed not from loss of innocence but from losing the war. "All the Gulf War proved," one Vietnam combat veteran said to me, "was that we Americans don't like to lose." But now we have the mysterious Gulf War syndrome which by 1995 afflicted more than thirty thousand of the five hundred and fifty thousand soldiers sent to the Gulf.[12] This syndrome is ushering in a new generation of veterans suffering a *gestalt* of soul-sickness nobody can explain and our officials want to deny. The strategy of reclaiming our innocence through yet more warfare did not work.

Existential verities are, indeed, revealed by war. War can teach its participants that life is short and fragile, that its challenges must be met with courage, that we are agents of both creation and destruction and so should act with wisdom, restraint, and compassion. These lessons are difficult to embrace even under the most generous cultural conditions. Yet far more than these existential verities of war are rendered invisible by American denial. America claims innocence as its fundamental character trait. "...[B]elief allowed them to go forward uncorrupted in the midst of dirty doings, untouched by their own shadow, innocent," James Hillman writes about characteristic American public figures. "...[I]t is precisely this American habit of belief that... must be the essence of the American character..."[13]

We can say the same about our veterans. As a culture we believe that our boys should be able "to go forward uncorrupted in the midst of dirty doings" and return home innocent and well. That is how the quintessential American war hero, John Wayne, portrayed the experience of warfare to generations of Americans. His importance as a cultural role model cannot be underestimated because he was just a movie star. One night soon after his arrival in Vietnam, one infantry veteran I worked with attended a movie screening at his base camp. He watched Yul Brynner in "The Magnificent Seven" shoot down evil banditos. Afterwards he declared to himself, "Now I know why I'm here." Every other Vietnam veteran I have worked with refers to John Wayne as a guiding image and model. "I was seduced by World War II and John Wayne movies."[14] Part of our American innocence is expressed in our Hollywood consciousness. We believe that as we redefine and remake both ourselves and life in the movies, so can we do to ourselves and life as we live it. The Hollywood enterprise replicates through technology the innocence of self creation, of the American Adam, at the beginning of history, free to start over on our own terms. Thus John Wayne could successfully avoid conscription during World War II, never serve in war or taste its true nature, yet through public performance of how he and we wish war to be, establish himself as the role model for American soldiers.

American servicemen were portrayed as coming home from World War II with no pain. The supposed minority of psychological casualties were hidden in the back wards of veterans' hospitals. But millions of people, indeed our entire society, seemed happy that the great adventure was over. America was proud of its successful participation in the worldwide battle against evil. It moved on to the good life as defined by consumerism, with only a nostalgic glance backwards for the lost adventures of youth.

Denial is certainly not a cultural habit limited to the Vietnam War. Rather denial accompanies our very practice of warfare as well as other social policies and actions. World War II veterans being treated generously at conflict's end is the historical exception rather than the rule for America's treatment of its returning veterans. Perhaps what was unique, even successful about the Vietnam War was that so many people, both veterans and non-veterans, screamed out against denial. "The capacity to deny, to remain innocent, to use belief as a protection against sophistications of every sort— intellectual, aesthetic, moral, psychological—keeps the American character from awakening," says Hillman.[15] The severity of Vietnam veterans' suffering with and symptoms of Post-traumatic Stress Disorder are in direct response and proportion to the enormity of our culture's denial of their pain. Post-traumatic Stress Disorder, in its archetypal sense, represents the anguish, dislocation and rage of the soul as it attempts to awaken from such massive denial.

The Vietnam War destroyed the veterans' innocence. This is so not just on the individual psychological dimension, which could be damaging enough in itself, but it is a necessary component of the passage to adulthood. Even more devastating was that the Vietnam War destroyed veterans' ability to participate in America's mystique of innocence. The war removed many veterans from participating or girding themselves in this essential American character trait. Among my clients an air force squadron commander realized we were the bad guys as he watched us napalm beautiful, virginal mountains along the Laotian border; an army truck driver realized it when he was ordered to exhume and relocate bodies of enemy dead with his back hoe; a machine gunner, as North Vietnamese were throwing themselves at his emplacement. In a flash, his weapon blazing, he saw that those we called enemies were human beings with families awaiting their return, yet willing to sacrifice their lives for a cause greater than themselves while all he wanted to do was get home in one piece, even if it meant killing them.

Recovering the times, places, and incidents during which the moral character and soul of a veteran awakened in the field is essential. The awakening is Janus-faced, looking simultaneously at both past and present, the found and the lost. In the field the marine found and lost himself at the same moment. Now at home and re-experiencing the war imaginally, he can reclaim the discovery of his soul and of a truthful moral order, fight fiercely to hold tightly to both soul and its code, and shape his adult years by that effort.

Veterans with Post-traumatic Stress Disorder are people with their personal and collective belief systems shattered. Such people are no longer innocent. They no longer believe that we or our actions, values, or policies are inherently good. Such people are, in an essential moral and spiritual sense, no longer American because they have left, abandoned, or felt banished from the American mythological context. "I'm not an American," one helicopter gunner who neither voted, paid taxes, nor obtained a driver's license, often said to me. "I'm a citizen of the underground."

It becomes clear why so many of the homeless on our urban streets, more than twenty or thirty per cent by some estimates, are Vietnam veterans. "On any given night, an estimated two hundred and seventy-one thousand of the nation's 26.4 million veterans are homeless," fifty-five to sixty percent of these having served during the Vietnam era.[16] Vietnam veterans in overwhelming numbers have been demonstrating to us that their war and homecoming experiences shattered their American belief systems, including their belief in their own goodness and innocence. This shattering, and not merely individual psychological dysfunction, did indeed render them homeless.

Homelessness is not merely an economic condition to be remedied by social programs. Rather homelessness is an archetypal condition in which the city, the state, not as historical nation but as *polis*, the essential political body of which we are an integral part, is not the proper and fit home for the individual. Socrates' friends offered him escape and exile when he was about to be sentenced to death. He refused. His soul could not leave its Athens home, and it would serve Athens even through death. Vietnam veterans, in contrast, tell us with their homelessness and post-traumatic stress disorder that their souls cannot come home to or be at home in America. They do not fit in a culture based on the belief in its own innocence and denial of its shadow, despite overwhelming evidence to the contrary; evidence with which the Vietnam veteran is painfully familiar.

III. The American Shadow in Vietnam

Images of the American shadow, fleeting glimpses of the mythic giant, fly by like tracers, glowing and bleeding against a green jungle backdrop. They bombard the psyche saturated with Vietnam battle scenes, enflame for a second and are gone before they can be grabbed. Regarding the Vietnam War, we are tempted to be like Cyclops, one-eyed, narrowed, dull-witted, and without peripheral vision. The chaotic nature and over-whelming pain of the war makes us not want to see it clearly. The shadow giant hides in shadowland.

With innocence and belief systems shattered by the brutality of technological warfare, the psychological and cultural containers of young men fighting in Vietnam were shattered. Two critical psychological events occurred. The shadow leaked, flowed, and exploded through many soldiers' psychological remnants. Then, without humanizing restraints, the warrior archetype became free to possess the soldier. The warrior archetype itself is not inherently brutal or sadistic and can be honorable and protective. However, sadism in war and life, according to Robert Moore, occurs when the ego has been shattered and the shadow warrior takes possession of the psyche.[17] Many young Americans in Vietnam became operatives of the American shadow. Veterans with Post-traumatic Stress Disorder still carry the moral stain and archetypal damage of war. They live in the shadow cast by the Shadow. The veteran, to rebuild his container and cleanse his soul, must become conscious of the dimensions of the mythic arena in which his soul was damaged. Where was he when he was in Vietnam? What war was he truly fighting? Here are some partial answers.

1. *Indian Country*

Enemy territory in Vietnam was known as "Indian Country." Numbered hills we killed and died for one day were given up the next; frightened or incompetent field officers; higher commanders making bets with soldiers' lives; learning to say "It don't mean nothing" as men looked upon their dead; burning and destroying people's homes, huts, livestock, gardens; poisoning and igniting entire forests and jungles; prostitution; black marketeering; drugs; rape; torture; body bags; mass executions of villagers; secret assassinations of political figures, no matter how large or small; fraggings and assassinations of our own people. This is not John Wayne behavior. Is this how Americans fight?

Think of the Vietnam War as the American frontier myth displaced to a virginal Asian forest among a people as different looking as were the Native Americans to our European ancestors, reenacted to its frenzied extreme, with attack helicopters and fighter planes for our cavalry horses and monstrously destructive weaponry for carbines and sabers. This is how Americans fight when we have not integrated the wounds of our own historical past but instead are given an undifferentiated mythic arena in which to reenact that past.

2. *"Waste them!"*

The code word combatants used to indicate killing was "waste." In military slang to waste was to kill an enemy. The word was quickly applied to any Vietnamese person or livestock. Soon to waste was to destroy a hut, a home, a village, a rice paddy, a mountain, a jungle. In Vietnam we attempted to waste an entire people and country.

Think of the Vietnam War as our consumer culture displaced to a jungle among people and a landscape not our own, with no rules or rituals to restrain or humanize it. As a result we were free to carry the shadow dimensions of consumerism—its blind, devouring hunger, its incessant making and disposing of waste— to its extreme. When we stopped fighting, we left behind the world's second largest military air force for the South Vietnamese. When we finally evacuated Saigon, we dumped much of it into the ocean. We are still paying the bills.

"Waste them" did not only refer to the Vietnamese. During the war American minorities and the poor were represented among our troops in numbers far beyond their proportion in the population. So we practiced the wasting of American youths. American draft practices began to empty the ghettoes and the hills. Those who did not fit into the American Dream were taken off our American streets where they might be a danger because of their disaffection. The Vietnam War occurred at the same time as the Civil Rights movement. The War in Asia heated up as did racial unrest at home. Think of the Vietnam War as population control, and as tear gas and water hoses on the ghettoes. The military has always been one of the few ways up and out of poverty and hopelessness in America. During Vietnam the way out was through fire.

And "waste them" referred to the treatment of veterans since returning from the war. No parades, no homecoming rituals, spit on at airports—these were the easy, surface signs. The long term neglect and ignorance is much more insidious.[18] For decades Agent Orange complaints were ridiculed by governmental authorities.[19] Veterans have been dispensed drugs at Veteran Administration hospitals as if they were at candy stores. Vets have shown me their computer printouts of their drug dispensation and intake histories; they read like the chemistry set experiments of mad scientists. In hospital, veterans were put in body coffins during flashbacks. By the late 1980s, more than sixty thousand veterans had committed suicide since returning from Vietnam, more than were killed during the entire war.[20] Imagine the black wall of names that is the Vietnam Memorial in Washington being more than twice the length it already is. If Post-traumatic Stress Disorder is the soul screaming its anguish, then America wastes the veterans carrying that anguish. Think of our treatment of Vietnam veterans since returning from the war as our collective attempt to kill the messenger.

IV. Emerging from the Shadow

James Hillman uses the word "accident" for those events that unexpectedly knock our souls off their projected course. Participation in war is a traumatic accident—unplanned, unexpected, and cosmological in its distortion and destruction of previous form. The archetypal approach to Post-traumatic Stress Disorder necessitates, in Hillman's words, that we

> keep accident as an authentic category of existence, forcing speculations about existence.... What does it mean, why did it happen, what does it want? Continuing reappraisals are part of the aftershock. The accident may never be integrated, but it may strengthen the integrity of the soul's form by adding to it perplexity, sensitivity, vulnerability, and scar tissue.[21]

The archetypal perspective reveals Post-traumatic Stress Disorder among Vietnam veterans to be many things. It is the shape of the soul's broken container due to its participation in unspeakably brutal modern warfare. It is the soul's cry of anguish. It is the moral stain the soul carries from being an operative of a cultural shadow. It is the soul's attempts to purge and cleanse. It is the ongoing shock of witness. It is the dislocation at returning to a culture denying such witness an audience and making war on the returned veterans' truths. It is the homelessness of the veterans' souls in a *polis* no longer their own. It is a troubled, incomplete presence in place of a dignified warrior archetype. It is continued possession by the shadow warrior archetype, because the returned soldier is no longer on a battlefield and is supposed to be civilized in a culture that does not grant a mature warrior identity to its veterans. It makes the carrier a walking, breathing symptom of the culture's soul sickness—a scar on the streets of a country that tries to deny its shadow and offers no rituals for containing yet expressing it. It becomes the identity of one who has participated in apocalypse and been abandoned there.

Effective psychotherapy for veterans with Post-traumatic Stress Disorder must address all these archetypal dimensions. Such therapy must include going on patrol with the veteran into the dark corners of the American shadow as they are revealed both in the jungles and at home. It must have the courage to stare into the horror of apocalypse. It must seek and gather the remnants of soul left there. It must discover how, when, where the soul awakened, protested, betrayed itself, went silent, became terrified, or numbed. It must effect a return that tends to the needs of returning warriors as traditional cultures did. It must offer the veteran the possibility of developing a new identity as an honorable returned warrior. Ultimately it must effect an imaginal initiation into a new form of warriorhood.

The warrior archetype in its mature condition helps an individual serve the community in truth. The mature warrior has witnessed to the horror and shadow and so can recognize it and help protect against its pathological outbreak. This is what the accident of war wants of its survivor. Only in this new identity can the soul that has survived modern war regain a necessary and life-affirming form and restore its integrity.

The archetype of the warrior is a necessary component of psyche and culture that cannot and should not be eradicated. Healing for veterans must consist of embracing the warrior archetype while cleansing it of its shadow dimensions. Healing for our world can occur only with the wisdom, restraint, and dark witness that mature warriors can offer.

Notes

[1] David Nichols, ed. *Ernie's War: The Best of Ernie Pyle's World War II Dispatches* (New York: Simon & Schuster, 1987), 87.

[2] James Hillman, *The Soul's Code: In Search of Character and Calling* (New York: Random House, 1996), 87.

[3] Richard Lattimore, tr. *Greek Lyrics* (Chicago: University of Chicago Press, 1960), 61.

[4] Jim Goodwin, "The Etiology of Combat-related Post-traumatic Stress Disorders," *Post-traumatic Stress Disorders: A Handbook for Clinicians*, Tom Williams, ed. (Cincinnati: Disabled American Veterans, 1987), 7.

[5]Goodwin, 8.

[6]Goodwin, 6-7.

[7]Goodwin, 8.

[8]Robert Jay Lifton, *Home From the War: Vietnam Veterans, Neither Victims Nor Executioners* (New York: Simon & Schuster, 1973).

[9]Gustav Hasford, *The Short Timers* (New York: Bantam, 1980), 55.

[10]Edward Tick, "Satori in the Hut," *Pilgrimage: Psychotherapy and Personal Exploration*, 19:3, Summer, 1993, 24-26.

[11]George Bush, *Presidential Diaries*, quoted in Herbert Parmet, *George Bush* (New York: Scribner's, 1997), 479.

[12]Eric Schmitt, "The Gulf War Veteran: Victorious in War, Not Yet at Peace," *The New York Times*, May 29, 1995. Sec. 4, 1.

[13]Hillman, 268.

[14]Mark Baker, *Nam: The Vietnam War in the Words of the Men and Women Who Fought There* (New York: William Morrow, 1981), 33. This quote is notable not for its uniqueness but for its commonality. Echoed by a vast majority of Vietnam veterans, it is a mantra of a media generation.

[15]Hillman, 268.

[16]Schmitt, Sec 4, 4.

[17]Robert Moore and Douglas Gillette, *The Warrior Within: Accessing the Knight in the Male Psyche* (New York: William Morrow, 1992), 132 ff.

[18]For a fuller treatment of the symptoms and consequences of such neglect, see Edward Tick, "Neglecting Our Vietnam Wounds," in *Voices: the Art and Science of Psychotherapy*, Spring, 1986, 22:1, 46-56.

[19]For an early yet definitive examination of the Agent Orange problem, see Fred A. Wilcox, *Waiting for an Army to Die: The Tragedy of Agent Orange* (New York: Vintage, 1983).

[20]W. H. Capps, *The Unfinished War: Vietnam and the American Conscience* (Boston: Beacon Press, 1982).

[21]Hillman, 207.

DESEGREGATING THE WHITE EGO: RACISM AND THE ETHIC OF WHITE CIVILIZATION

MICHAEL VANNOY ADAMS

A year ago, during the professional football season, a friend of mine who lives in Dallas telephoned me after one of the Cowboys' victories. Although the Cowboys had won that game, my friend was concerned that they might not make it into the playoffs, let alone to the Super Bowl. He was worried, he told me, that, as he put it, "our niggers" would let us down.

I grew up in Bonham, a small town in Texas, eighty miles northeast of Dallas. I entered first grade in 1954, the year of the *Brown v. Board of Education* Supreme Court decision. White students attended the "Bonham" schools; black students, the "Booker T. Washington" school. Not until my senior year was Bonham High School finally desegregated. I started playing football in junior high school in 1960, the very year that the Cowboys started playing in Dallas. My friend also grew up in Bonham. We played together on the high school football team,

Michael Vannoy Adams, D.Phil., C.S.W., is an analytical psychologist in private practice in New York City. He is the author of *The Multicultural Imagination: Race, Color, and the Unconscious*, London and New York: Routledge, 1996.

and we became Cowboy fans. We learned to love Tom Landry's
Cowboys and hate Vince Lombardi's Green Bay Packers.

Our high school team was good enough one year to make it
into the playoffs, where we lost to the eventual state champions, a
team with an ambidextrous quarterback who astonished us by
throwing passes both right- and left-handed. Then our team
suddenly achieved a certain inadvertent notoriety. After the
season, at the banquet where we received our varsity letter jackets,
the professional football player who delivered the usual inspirational
speech also presented each of us with a small book of religious
testimonials by members of the Fellowship of Christian Athletes.
A few weeks later, a fan of some rival team (may he burn eternally
in hell) anonymously reported the gift to the Texas Interscholastic
League, which ruled that we had technically exceeded the monetary
limit on the value of awards and that we would therefore be
ineligible for the playoffs the next season no matter how many
games we might win. As the newspapers erroneously inflated the
story, we had been penalized for accepting Bibles. Long before the
Dallas Cowboys became "America's Team," we were, for all the good
it did us, "God's Team."

In "Ball/Play," the Jungian analyst Ronald Schenk says that
playing ball, including football, was for him, too (although in a
more positive sense), "a religious experience." The "ball player"
was an archetype with which he identified heroically, until, that is,
he reached what he calls "my level of incompetence in four
traumatically unsuccessful years of football at a major college"
(1994: 17-18), after which he had a series of recurrent, post-
traumatic dreams that finally enabled him to disidentify from the
archetype of the ball player. As I have noted in "Metaphors in
Psychoanalytic Theory and Therapy" (Adams, 1997), football is
an example of the "game of life" metaphor that the unconscious
sometimes employs.

My Texan friend and I go back a long way. We have continued
to be friends over the years largely because of the Cowboys.
Although I now live in New York City, I do not root for the
Giants or the Jets. I remain loyal to the Cowboys. If my friend and
I now have little else in common, we still have the Cowboys to

talk about. The folklorist Alan Dundes has written a humorously satirical psychoanalytic essay on American football. As Dundes interprets football, it is a masculine, phallic-anal ritual in which the players engage in symbolic "homosexual" sport; one team attempts to "score" by penetrating the "endzone" of the other team (1980). According to this interpretation, we Dallas fans are "drugstore cowboys" for whom football is a form of male, homoerotic bonding. It is a way for us to feel "manly" solidarity, even if only through television, and after the game, over the telephone.

How did I react to my friend's reference to "our niggers?" Although I felt dismay, I let the remark pass in silence. What kind of friend am I and to whom? Did I owe it to my black friends to challenge my white friend? It was not the first time that I have heard him or other old Texan friends use the "n-word." Should I have reacted with a vocal protest on this or previous occasions? What good, I ask myself, would it have done if I had? My old Texan friends all have university educations; they are all professionals; politically, they prefer to vote Democrat; most of them are liberals. I have never witnessed any of them engage in any form of actual invidious discrimination on the basis of "race" or color; nor do I believe that they would. Yet they continue, on occasion, to use the word "nigger." They do not, of course, use it around blacks, only around other whites. I conclude that they *like* to use it. Saying "nigger" gives them pleasure and a peculiar sense of solidarity in a collective "racial" identity. I have the impression that they consider it their "right" to say the word and that they are adamant that nobody is going to tell them not to say it.

To my Texan friend, Green Bay Packer fans may have their black players—Mike Holmgren, the Packers' coach imports soul food and an African-American barber from Milwaukee—but we Dallas Cowboy fans also have our black players. My friend is worried because he knows very well that our team cannot win without our black players. He has in mind not only Emmitt Smith and Michael Irvin but also the vast majority of the starting players on both offense and defense. Does not Barry Switzer, the Cowboys' coach, have a reputation for knowing how to relate with sensitivity to black players? Has Charles Haley not said as much? Do black players require special handling?

What does the word "nigger" mean to my friend? In this instance, it means someone who is liable to let us down. How, exactly, would "our niggers" let us down? They would let us down by lying down—by not giving, as football coaches are fond of saying hyperbolically, 110 percent effort. The notion is that blacks are more likely than whites like "us" to lie down on the job: that blacks have less of a work ethic than whites. Never mind that there is no evidence that Troy Aikman works harder than Emmitt Smith and Michael Irvin do. Troy would never let us down because he is one of "us." Other players may suffer ennui during the regular season, but not Troy, who said after the Cowboys' first playoff victory, "I hoped it was the case that this team was bored in the regular season. We realize that the regular season really doesn't matter and we're judged on how we do in the playoffs. I don't think it's right, but we do have some players that get bored with the regular season" (*George*, 29 December 1996: 8, 3). Who, I wonder, could these players be? Troy remains excited and stays focused no matter what; others get bored. Could these others be "our niggers?"

Leo Stone has written a famous psychoanalytic essay entitled "On the Principal Obscene Word of the English Language" (1984). Stone has in mind the "f-word." African-Americans, of course, might have quite another candidate in mind for the principal obscene word. They do not need O. J. Simpson and Mark Fuhrman to remind them of what it might be. To a Freudian analyst, with sex on the theoretical brain, "fuck" seems more obscene than any other word in the English language. To an African-American, however, "nigger" is the most obscene.

When my Texan friend and I were playing football together in high school, Dan Jenkins was covering the Cowboys as a sportswriter for the *Dallas Morning News*. Later—it is now twenty-five years ago—Jenkins wrote a novel, *Semi-Tough* (1972), about professional football, which my friend and I both read. The novel was eventually made into a movie starring Kris Kristofferson, Burt Reynolds, and Jill Clayburgh. At the very beginning of the novel, the main character, a white football player from Texas, Billy Clyde Puckett, defends his use of the "n-word":

And let me get something straight right away which bothers me. Just because I may happen to say nigger doesn't mean that I'm some kind of racist. One of the big troubles with the world of modern times, I think, is that somebody is always getting hot because somebody else says nigger instead of nee-grow.

Because of this very thing I said nigger just now to get your attention. It seems to have a certain shock value. But I don't think nigger in my heart. Not the way some people do when they mean a nigger is a lazy sumbitch who won't block or tackle or wash dishes fast enough.

It's just a word, anyway. Nigger, I mean. It's just a word that some dumb-ass plantation owner made up one time by accident when he tried to pronounce nee-grow. (4)

Billy Clyde goes on to say that, as far as he is concerned, football players, white or black, are just football players and that he knows several blacks "who can block and tackle themselves pretty damn white" (4). He then relates how his white teammate and best friend, Shake Tiller, also a Texan, once addressed the black players, including Puddin Patterson, at a team meeting: "'I'm gonna catch the football and run like a nigger, Puddin. You gonna block yourself white?'" Shake says that the team can win only if the white and black players win together. Puddin replies: "'Everybody wants that, baby, but you sound like you think that if we don't win, it's gonna be the cats that fucked it up. You dig that?'" Shake grins and says: "'That's because we all know how lazy you folks are'" (12-13). He smiles when he says that, in order to let the black players know that he means it not literally but ironically. In spite of some tension, Puddin and the other black players decide not to take offense at this white appeal for team unity. The novel employs a "racial" epithet to satirize white-black relations, but it also documents, quite accurately, certain white attitudes toward blacks—and these are not just the attitudes of some white Texans; they are the attitudes of many white Americans.

When I began to write my book, *The Multicultural Imagination*, I was impressed by the paucity of references to "race" or "racism" in the indexes of psychoanalytic books and journals. References to anti-Semitism were the sole exception to this rule. There are, of course, many Jewish psychoanalysts and very few black psychoanalysts. Historically many Freudian analysts have also had a special interest in sexuality. For Freud, the unconscious was predominantly a "sexual" unconscious. Few analysts—Freudian, Jungian, or otherwise—have evinced much interest in what I call the "raciality" of the unconscious. I do not mean to imply that different "races" have biologically different psyches. Such an assumption would be a racist notion. Contrary to what some biologists still maintain (King 1981), I do not believe that *races*, as such, even exist. (Racism, of course, does exist.) "Racial" (in contrast to genetic) categorizations are not natural facts but cultural artifacts, or constructs, which are arbitrary. That is why I always place the word "race" within quotation marks. By the "raciality" of the unconscious, I merely mean to emphasize, for example, that sexual issues are neither the only nor necessarily the most important contents of the unconscious. To some of us—including some patients—"racial" issues are also extremely significant contents.

Ernest Jones, Freud's biographer, also wrote an essay on obscenity. In "A Linguistic Factor in English Characterology" (1951), Jones, like Stone, emphasizes sexuality. According to Jones the characteristic propriety, or prudery, of the English is in part either a cause or an effect of linguistic repression or euphemism. He notes that, historically, Saxon words for "sexual" organs have been replaced by Norman words, which in turn have been replaced by Latin words. In polite English company, for example, the Saxon word "gut" was replaced by the Norman word "bowel," which was replaced by the Latin word "intestine."

It is not only the English, however, but also we Americans who replace certain words with others. The lower-case "negro" was replaced by the upper-case "Negro," which was replaced by the lower-case "black," which was replaced by the upper-case "Black," which was replaced by "Afro-American," which was replaced by "African-American"—and "colored person" has been replaced by "person of color." Just as "gut" has been repressed, so has "nigger"—except when some whites speak to other whites, or when some blacks speak to other blacks—or when some whites speak to blacks with an obscene or offensive intent.

I would emphasize that skin, white or black, is also an organ. It is not Freud or Jung but Alfred Adler who analyzes the organic. He does so in terms of inferiority and superiority. According to Adler, the "inferiority complex" has an organic basis (1916). We may have—or we may imagine that we have—an inferior organ. A sense of physical inferiority results in a sense of psychical inferiority. In racist color-coding, white skin is superior and black skin inferior. It is not the color of the skin as such, however, but what it ostensibly indicates that is the decisive issue. For racists, the skin is an external, surface appearance, the color of which is an indicator of an internal, depth reality, or "essence." What is the essence of "white" and "black?" For my friend, white skin indicates industry; black skin, indolence. Ultimately, he has no confidence that in the fourth quarter, when, as football coaches like to say, it is time for a "gut check" (or should it be an "intestine check?") players with black skin will respond with fortitude equal to that of players with white skin.

How does my Texan friend reach such a conclusion? It seems obvious to me that it is a consequence not of any direct, personal experience of blacks but rather of an indirect, collective notion about them. His worry that "our niggers" will let us down is a product of the *cultural unconscious* or, more specifically, the *white* cultural unconscious. By the "cultural unconscious" I mean the forms and contents, the stereotypes and stereotypical images, whether they be honorific or defamatory, that are *culturally ingrained* in us (Adams 1991: 253). The color complex of whites is a "superiority complex." In the cultural unconscious of whites, the collective notion is that blacks are primitive and instinctive, while whites are civilized and rational. In *The Multicultural Imagination*, I argue that a certain Eurocentric, ethnocentric "logic" opposes the associations "white," "civilized," and "rational" to the associations "black," "primitive," and "instinctive," and then judgmentally proclaims the one to be superior and the other inferior (Adams 1996: 52). This, to me, is the gist of white supremacy. It is also one of the main variations on the theme of the mind-body split which, for Freudians, is an ego-id split, and for Jungians, an ego-shadow split: whites are more conscious; blacks, less conscious—even, at the extreme, utterly unconscious. My psychoanalytic research into the origins of racism has led me to inquire into what whites imagine about blacks. My Texan friend imagines that, when push finally comes to shove on the football field, "our niggers" may prove unreliable. In what does this unreliability consist? In my friend's fantasy, blacks have a more "primitive" attitude than whites. They are more undisciplined or less repressed. The notion is that, at some moment in history, whites became "civilized." In contrast blacks are, at worst, "uncivilized," or at best, "semi-civilized." Blacks have not yet attained the stage of civilization that whites have achieved.

From a psychoanalytic perspective, this fantasy entails the proposition that blacks have a less phylogenetically evolved or ontogenetically developed ego than whites have. What, however, do we mean by the ego? As Freud defines "ego," it is "reason" in relation to the "reality principle." For Freudians to have an ego is to be rational and realistic. This definition seems to me to beg an absolutely crucial question, for it does not adequately take into account the fact that history conditions how we define "ego." "Ego" simply means "I," and the specific content of our sense of "I-ness" is not invariant. The content varies historically. The ego is a variable not a constant. I would emphasize that, in pure theory, *the ego is an empty place holder* in our personal equation. Since the Enlightenment or Age of Reason, however, it has seemed to some of us—including Freud—that our sense of "I-ness," our very identity, is or should be, identical with "reason." Freud thus arbitrarily privileges reason over all other potential contents of the ego. Anything else, everything else, is "unreason" which we need to repress—or perhaps sublimate. From this perspective some of us—we whites—have historically repressed unreason and identified with reason. What, however, do we mean by "reason?" Is it rationality or mere rationalization?

I would say that "reason" is an *ethic*. I do not mean that to be rational is to be "ethical." I mean that reason is an "ethic" in the sense that historically it implies certain collective cultural values (or "virtues") in the sense that Max Weber defines the term in *The Protestant Ethic and the Spirit of Capitalism* (1992). It is also important to acknowledge that, as Weber says, "what is rational from one point of view may well be irrational from another" (26). What one categorizes as "reason" or "unreason" depends on one's perspective. For my friend who worries about "our niggers" letting us down, this ego ethic includes a work ethic which he imagines that blacks have not completely adopted as whites presumably have. The implicit assumption is that blacks still have a "slave mentality"— the contemporary version of which is a "welfare mentality"—rather than a work ethic. The notion is that, in contrast to whites, blacks lack an internal motivation to work. Blacks work if forced to do so, as when they were enslaved; if not, they remain unmotivated— even, at the extreme, unemployed. In my friend's fantasy, when the going gets tough, "our niggers" will be only "semi-tough;" they will no longer repress the contents of the id or shadow—instinctive or inferior tendencies—but will regress to a primitive condition that whites have more or less permanently superseded, evolutionarily or developmentally. In *Darwin's Athletes: How Sport Has Damaged Black America and Preserved the Myth of Race,* John Hoberman notes that, historically, whites have always questioned whether blacks, in a confrontation with adversity, possess "what modern coaches call 'mental toughness'" (1997: 68-9).

Why should this fantasy so exercise whites like my friend? In *Civilization and Its Discontents* (1930/1961) Freud argues that to be civilized is, by definition, to be "discontented." If we are civilized, we are discontented, he says because we are repressed. We have had to repudiate every tendency that seems to be incompatible with civilization. For Freud the most important repression in the service of civilization is a renunciation of immediate sexual gratification. Sexual restraint is certainly one of the main elements in the fantasy of white civilization. It is, however, I would maintain, only one of the elements and not necessarily the most significant.

What are the distinctive features of the contemporary fantasy of white Americans about black Americans? I would emphasize three features (although I might mention others): sex, drugs, and guns. Many, if not most, white Americans imagine that black Americans—especially black American men—have an inordinate proclivity for sex, drugs, and guns. This fantasy extends to more than underclass blacks in some innercity ghetto. Michael Irvin, the multimillionaire star black player was suspended from the Dallas Cowboys for five games during the 1996 football season after he pleaded no contest to felony cocaine possession and misdemeanor marijuana possession in the presence of "models" in a hotel room. He was later accused of holding a gun to the head of a woman at this party while another black player raped her. No formal charges were ever filed, and Irvin and the other player were eventually publicly exonerated by the Dallas police (Verhovek, 13 January 1997: C, 4). As a result Michael Irvin is only one of a number of black men who seem to some whites to confirm the "truth" of this fantasy. The contemporary opposition between the civilized and the primitive, between "white" and "black," thus includes abstinence versus promiscuity, sobriety versus intoxication, and gentility versus violence. Apparently, no matter how many whites indulge in sex, drugs, and guns, that behavior does not refute the fantasy of some whites that blacks are more susceptible to such "vices." These whites simply continue to assume the worst of blacks.

If I were to summarize the oppositions of abstinence versus promiscuity, sobriety versus intoxication, and gentility versus violence, I would say that they amount to an opposition between composure and impulsivity. In conversations with a black friend, a psychoanalyst, I have been struck by the number of anecdotes he tells about having been in situations in which his ability to control his impulses has been seriously questioned by whites. Over and over again, whites expect him—in fact, they attempt to provoke him—to "act out." It is as if they desperately need him to validate a stereotype or stereotypical image of the out-of-control black in opposition to the in-control white.

On one occasion I remarked to my black psychoanalyst friend that white fantasies about black intelligence—or the lack thereof—seemed to me even more pernicious than white fantasies about black sexuality. He agreed with me, and I was not surprised that he did so. I do believe that many whites tend to imagine that blacks are mentally inferior (and physically superior). *The Bell Curve: Intelligence and Class Structure in American Life,* by Richard J. Herrnstein and Charles Murray (1994), is only the most recent effort to prove that blacks are "racially" less intelligent than whites. The opposition between the civilized and the primitive thus also includes intelligence versus stupidity or knowledge versus ignorance. Whites are intelligent or knowledgable; blacks are stupid or ignorant.

What I call the white "ethic" thus consists of a set of cultural values or notions about white "discipline": industry, abstinence, sobriety, gentility, composure, intelligence, and knowledge versus indolence, promiscuity, intoxication, violence, impulsivity, stupidity, and ignorance. As what I call an "other-image," blacks thus pose a dire threat to the self-image of whites. They also, however, serve another purpose, an opportunistic one. If blacks did not exist, whites would have to invent them for they function as a convenient excuse onto which whites can project all of the aspects of the id or shadow that the ego represses or otherwise excludes from consideration. The existence of putatively instinctive and inferior blacks provides an opportunity for whites to pretend that they are rational and superior.

Historically the white ethic is an incredibly ambitious cultural project. It is also a problematic one. Blacks have paid a terrible price for the pretensions of whites, and whites know very well that they have exacted this price from blacks. Then is it any wonder that whites are afraid of blacks? A year or so ago, one of my black friends remarked to me that I am the only white man he has known who has not seemed to be afraid of being around black men. I must say that this observation startled me. I *suppose* that I felt complimented, but at the same time I felt immensely saddened, for I suddenly imagined what it is to be not someone who *fears* but someone who *is feared*, constantly. To be feared seemed to me much more horrible than to fear, for someone who is afraid of me can be extremely dangerous to me. Someone might *do* something to me simply because he is so afraid of me.

What, exactly, are whites afraid of? I believe that whites feel great unconscious guilt over the ways in which they have persecuted and exploited blacks historically. Whites have projected onto blacks (whom they have oppressed) those instinctive and inferior qualities that they have repressed. Whites fear not so much what Freud calls "the return of the repressed" as they fear what I would call *the return of the oppressed*. If the historical roles had been reversed, if whites instead of blacks had been victimized by slavery and segregation, would they not now retaliate or revolt with a vengeance? I believe that whites, perhaps especially white men, are afraid of blacks because they feel that blacks would be perfectly justified in a massive, collective retribution against whites. I also believe that at least some whites fear that blacks, given the opportunity, might eventually demonstrate that they are not only physically superior to whites but also mentally superior—and that therefore they must be denied that opportunity.

I would also mention the "Cress theory" of white supremacy. In *The Isis Papers: The Keys to the Colors* (1991), Frances Cress Welsing proposes a genetic explanation of why whites are so afraid of blacks. Although the book is an example of what Freud condemns as "wild analysis" (1910/1957)—Welsing is a case of a crackpot calling the kettle white—she does say, quite correctly, that we need to analyze "the underlying psychodynamics of the collective white psyche and of the white supremacy power system and its culture" (103). As eccentric as her particular interpretations are—they are often vulgar applications of Freudian theory—her general assertion that whites are collectively afraid of blacks because they are unconsciously afraid of "genetic annihilation" through miscegenation, or "interracial" sexual intercourse and procreation, requires serious consideration. Is there some sense in which whites are profoundly afraid of the loss of a "racially" pure identity through a genetic mixture of the dominant color "black" with the recessive color "white?" According to Welsing, whites fear that blacks will render them extinct as a "race"—as Ernest Jones reports that Freud once predicted they eventually would, at least in America (1955 2: 60).

Not only blacks but also whites have paid a price in the name of civilization. Whether whites are actually more repressed—and more discontented—than blacks, they tend to imagine that they are. They imagine that the price of civilization is a certain deprivation. When the going gets tough, whites would like to lie down on the job, but they have to pretend that they have no such propensity. To admit as much would be to imagine the end of civilization as they know it. I believe that whites resent blacks because they envy what they regard as a license to behave in ways that they have repressed and must continue to repress in order to preserve civilization. In the white imagination, blacks are simultaneously both a threat and a temptation. The white ego or "reason," which is an ethic of collective white values, feels threatened by "unreason" (which whites unconsciously color-code as "black") precisely because it feels tempted by the white id or white shadow. In some secret recess of the white unconscious, whites would like nothing more than to behave licentiously, to express the instinctive and inferior qualities that they impute to blacks, but because historically they have assumed what they regard as responsibility for the very existence of civilization, they feel that they cannot. If they did, they would no longer be "white."

This "obligation" to sustain civilization used to be called, of course, "the white man's burden." I believe that whites do feel burdened by civilization and that they want blacks to get off their backs. Shortly after *The Multicultural Imagination* was published, a psychoanalyst friend of mine, a white woman, said to me, "In the current situation, your book may actually sell." The implication was that if it were not for "the current situation," no one would buy my book. What did she mean by "the current situation?" I sensed that she meant that if blacks had not so exaggerated the magnitude and extent of racism, then there would be no market for a book such as mine. In the present circumstance, any demand for a book like mine would merely be artificial.

If my interpretation of her remark was correct, my psychoanalyst friend is one of those whites—and there are many—who feel that blacks should stop complaining about racism, for they really have nothing, or nothing much, any longer to complain about. The 1950s and 1960s promised much, perhaps too much, in regard to racism. Those were the years of desegregation, civil rights protests, and "Great Society" programs. The results have disappointed many whites and many blacks. Why anyone, white or black, should have imagined that these recent efforts, as sincere and serious as they were, should have solved the problem after four hundred years of racism in America is, of course, a commentary on just how naive the expectations were. We seem always to be impatient for a quick fix. There is now a reaction, or a backlash, a certain cynicism on the part of many whites, who feel that they have done quite enough for blacks and that blacks should now shoulder their fair share of the burden of civilization. Jung had a fancy word for this process—*enantiodromia*—by which he meant a pendulum swing of opinion from one extreme to the opposite extreme. Whites like my psychoanalyst friend have swung from a liberal position on racism to a reactionary position. She may not be a football fan, but she is just as disappointed in "our niggers" as my Texan friend is.

Jung entitled one of his books *Modern Man in Search of a Soul*. I believe that modern white man needs to do some soul-searching. What Jung had to say about the ego was different from what Freud had to say about it. As Jung defines "ego," it is not reason in relation to the reality principle. The ego is simply whatever attitude the "I" happens to be identified with at any one time. (It may, of course, be identified with "reason," but that is by no means the only possibility.) According to Jung, the attitude of the ego is always partial, prejudicial, even—at the extreme—utterly defective. He says the function of the unconscious is to compensate the conceits of the ego which represses, ignores, neglects, or otherwise excludes from consideration other possible contents, often for defensive purposes. The unconscious presents for consideration various alternative perspectives that the ego may then entertain: contents that the ego may evaluate and then decide either to accept or reject. If the ego is receptive rather than defensive, it may integrate at least some of these contents. Uncritical resistance to integrating such contents is a variety of psychical "apartheid;" the segregation of contents apart from the ego. What we need is *desegregation of the white ego*.

The unconscious functions to relativize the ego, to demonstrate that the identifications of the ego are not absolute but always relative to certain ideals (among them collective cultural values— what I call an ethic). In this sense the identifications of the ego are idealizations of what I believe "I" am or should be—in exclusionary opposition to what I believe "I" am *not* or should *not* be. When ego is split from id or when ego is split from shadow, those unconscious contents that we quite literally *denigrate* and then dissociate from our self-image are our "other-images:" it is these unconscious contents that are "*our* niggers," the images of *our* instincts, the images of *our* inferiorities. As long as we whites refuse to search our souls or analyze our psyches, these contents will lurk in the unconscious and then suddenly return, symptomatically, with all the vengeance of indolence, promiscuity, intoxication, violence, impulsivity, stupidity, and ignorance.

We tend to take culture for granted. Certain cultural attitudes are so unconsciously ingrained in us—we are so unconsciously habituated to them—that they seem "natural." These attitudes seem "second nature" when in actuality they are nothing more nor less than what they are—culture. Fundamentally culture consists of mores; collective habits that are not necessary but conventional and contingent. These include "habits of mind"—collective attitudes with which we are identified—and I would emphasize, from which we can disidentify and to which we can then relate in a new and different, critically reflective way.

My Texan friend was right to worry. The Cowboys did not make it to the Super Bowl that year. The Green Bay Packers did, and they won. The Cowboys were eliminated in the second playoff game. On twenty-two carries, Emmitt Smith gained 80 yards. After catching a pass on only the Cowboys' second offensive play, Michael Irvin was tackled so hard that he was removed from the game because it was feared that his collarbone had been broken. Troy Aikman threw three pass interceptions. My friend did not telephone to complain that "our niggers" had let us down. This time, there was no convenient excuse, no obvious scapegoat—no black players onto which a white fan could complacently and facilely project the id or shadow, the instinctive or inferior inclinations that exist in the white cultural unconscious.

Such a moment presents an occasion for critical reflection and a deconstruction and transvaluation of psychical values (which include cultural values). When the experience of external reality does not conform to what my Texan friend calls his "worry," when in fact it conflicts with it, he has an opportunity to reconsider just how partial, prejudicial, even defective his egocentric attitude is, just how extreme his white cultural ethic is. Not only the unconscious but also an experience of external reality can have a compensatory, integrative function. What my Texan friend needs to worry about is not whether the Cowboys will make it to another Super Bowl or whether the black players on the team will let him down, but how his ego needs to be less defensive against and more receptive to alternative perspectives that contradict and discredit his bigotry. And whether when he says "nigger," he thinks "nigger" in his heart. We all have our biases, by no means all of which are "racial." The value of psychoanalysis—and especially of Jungian analysis—is that it offers a theory and a method for exposing them, confronting them, and transforming them.

Works Cited

Adams, Michael V. "My Siegfried Problem—And Ours: Jungians, Freudians, Anti-Semitism, and the Psychology of Knowledge." In A. Maidenbaum and S. A. Martin (eds.), *Lingering Shadows: Jungians, Freudians, and Anti-Semitism*. Boston: Shambhala, 1991.

_____. *The Multicultural Imagination: "Race," Color, and the Unconscious*. London: Routledge, 1996.

_____. "Metaphors in Psychoanalytic Theory and Therapy." *Clinical Social Work Journal*, 5, 1: 27-39, 1997.

Adler, Alfred. *The Neurotic Constitution: Outlines of a Comparative Individualistic Psychology and Psychopathology*. Trans. B. Glueck and J. E. Lind. New York: Moffat, Yard, 1916.

Dundes, Alan. "Into the Endzone for a Touchdown: A Psychoanalytic Consideration of American Football." In *Interpreting Folklore*. Bloomington, Ind.: Indiana UP, 1980.

Freud, Sigmund. "Wild Psycho-analysis." *SE* 12: 219-27, 1910/1957.

_____. "Civilization and Its Discontents." *SE* 21: 57-145, 1930/1961.

George, T. "Romping Dallas Shows It's Far from Finished," *New York Times*, 8, 1 and 3. December 29, 1996.

Herrnstein, Richard J., and Murray, Charles. *The Bell Curve: Intelligence and Class Structure in American Life*. New York: Free Press, 1994.

Hoberman, John. *Darwin's Athletes: How Sport Has Managed Black America and Preserved the Myth of Race*. New York: Houghton Mifflin, 1997.

Jenkins, Dan. *Semi-Tough*. New York: Atheneum, 1972.

Jones, Ernest. "A Linguistic Factor in English Characterology." In *Essays in Applied Psycho-analysis*. London: Hogarth Press, 1951.

_____. *The Life and Work of Sigmund Freud: Years of Maturity, 1901-1919*. Vol. 2. New York: Basic Books, 1955.

King, J. C. *The Biology of Race*. Berkeley, Calif.: University of California Press, 1981.

Schenk, Ronald. "Ball/Play." In Murray Stein and John Hollowitz (eds.), *Psyche and Sports*. Wilmette, Ill.: Chiron, 1994.

Stone, L. "On the Principal Obscene Word of the English Language." In *Transference and Its Context: Selected Papers on Psychoanalysis*. New York: Jason Aronson, 1984.

Verhovek, S. H. "A Woman's False Accusation Prompts Reflection," *New York Times*, C, 4. January 13, 1997.

Weber, Max. *The Protestant Ethic and the Spirit of Capitalism*. Trans. T. Parsons. London: Routledge, 1992.

Welsing, Frances C. *The Isis Papers: The Keys to the Colors*. Chicago: Third World Press, 1991.

RE-SINK THE TITANIC

GLEN SLATER

> Western man has no need of more superiority over na-
> ture, whether outside or inside. He has both in almost
> devilish perfection. What he lacks is conscious recognition
> of his inferiority to the nature around and within him. He
> must learn that he may not do exactly as he wills. If he does
> not learn this, his own nature will destroy him.
> — C. G. Jung, *CW* § 535

At the bottom of the sea, somewhere between the Old
World and the New, a giant sleeps. It is a final, deathly
sleep, though not a peaceful one; the demise was too
sudden, the shock too great, the consequences too much to
assimilate. Contrasting the image of her motionless bulk, the
dreaming remains restless. The Titanic, yet to find her place in
the underworld, exists between worlds, waiting upon some
gesture, remembrance, or ritual. The broken waters of a calm,
clear night early this century still stir the imagination and wait
upon soulful attendance. Between fact and fiction, history and
myth, this once celebrated Titaness lingers. Our response to
her cry has been fervent, but not very insightful. We have

Glen Slater, Ph.D., is the Dissertation Coordinator in the Clinical Psychology
program, Pacifica Graduate Institute, Santa Barbara, California.

searched for her broken body, pondered the circumstances of her demise, retold her story and that of those who anchored her fate. More recently we have mapped out her murky location, photographed her through a deep blue shroud, and irreverently removed her belongings. Still, Titanic sleeps uneasily, and we are a part of her restless dreaming.

The Titanic disaster of April 15, 1912, is singular among modern catastrophes for its hold on the collective psyche. As the largest steamship of her time, longer, taller, heavier than anything else afloat, a technological marvel without precedent, Titanic ferried the visions of a modern industrial age. As an icon of technological disaster, painfully checking the flight of this modern bearing, we turn to her story for historical perspective. And as a messenger to a culture continuing to ignore nature's warnings, we still live within Titanic's wake. Eighty-five years after the event, books, documentaries, feature films, and even a Broadway musical bear witness to this unfinished dream.

When the technology arrived, fascination with the disaster turned into literally dredging. The exploration and museum plans made way for corporate-sponsored treasure hunts and salvage expeditions. Recently such exploits provided a spectacle for cruise ships which circled like sharks awaiting the arrival of each disemboweled section (Broad, 1996). But as superficial exploits increase and fascination turns to titillation, the disaster's unplumbed poignancy is only underscored. Although the ship herself has plunged into the deep, we have not yet made the accompanying descent. Submarines make it down but our reflections on the tragedy do not. We have not soulfully remembered Titanic's broken body. The autopsy has not yet progressed to a funereal rite. The dream has not been worked.

Our cultural attachment to the disaster resembles an obsession with an open wound, and has all the characteristics of an unrecognized cultural complex. We are compelled to get to the bottom of the literal reality, immersing ourselves in facts and theories; we want to see, touch, unravel, control. But, at its core, we cannot loosen the intensity of the initial devastation. Caught in a spell, chased by images, we are unable to assimilate the event's impact.

With each revisit little seems to change. The story is the same one, we know it backwards, and yet it continues to hold something. The pull does not subside. The event penetrates our vitals, but that which is vital consistently escapes. So we keep searching for the one thing we have overlooked all along—the memory that has not surfaced, the missing piece of evidence, the things that might have gone differently. The combination of this obsessive-compulsive attachment and the failure to honor Titanic in her dying suggests that within our dreaming there is also haunting. Here spectacle hides specter. Caught on the wrong level, our shallow remembering lays little to rest.

The task this dreaming and haunting presents is one of finding ears to listen and eyes to see; we need a fitting mode of perception. This is psyche's balm. When a traumatic experience rocks the soul, only the soul's forms and languages will be sufficient to digest the disturbance; when caught in a dream, we must follow the ways of the dream; when haunted, we must turn to the underworld. Technological analysis, recounting of facts, and photographing evidence will not do. A psychological salvage must be undertaken. This salvage attempt will explore our obsession with history's most significant maritime disaster through mythic forms, locating submerged fragments by following currents of poesis, reconfiguring the story from a soul perspective. Such an attempt will anchor itself to those points where the Titanic corresponds to modern crises and pathologies. Making this dive into the depths, attending to this level of complexity, would, I believe, mitigate the compulsion to drag concrete fragments of twisted wreckage to the surface. Witnessing the ship as she lies, locating her story within that of the modern era, its unconscious complexes and their archetypal roots, would forge an understanding that Titanic has a resting place. It is we who have not yet completed this voyage.

The Grip of a Titan

The ship and her story suggest a powerful but largely unrecognized mytheme at work in the culture. Recently, when an eleven ton section of Titanic's hull was nearing the surface, it broke loose and returned to the ocean floor (Broad, 1996, 6). Here psyche exercises her own intentionality: Opposing the great twentieth-century exploit of dragging everything into bright light, this event issues the decree that some things belong in the deep dark. At the very least it suggests an invitation for deepening and reflection—a need to take pause before action. But even the poesis of this moment and its invitation for introspection is avoided: Both the mechanical analysis of what went wrong and the counter-pole declaration that "the wreck is cursed" miss the boat. Both the scientific-technological attitude and the New Age seductions of curse and karma prevent the psychological salvage (although the fantasy of a curse may surely be taken as a sign of sacrilegious arrogance). Both the rational explanation and the metaphysical speculation remain unconsciously bound to the mytheme—caught in the headlock of an unnamed archetypal presence.

A major site of insight recovery stares us in the face. The archetypal character of the tragic event is already there in the ship's name. As architects of hubris—unmitigated pride and sacrilege—the Titans, a race of giants, fought with and were defeated by the Olympian gods then banished to the underworld. The root meaning of "hubris" suggests a "running riot" over other cosmic principles. The term "Titanic" refers originally to the temper of the war between the Titans and the Olympians. The Olympians, of course, portray the dominating forces of the cosmos, and personify the very organs of psychological life. Ever poised to displace this organicity, the Titans sponsor the gigantism of the psyche—inflation, grandiosity, unchecked haste. The myth suggests that identification with the Titanic tendency results in a heady power-trip followed by certain descent. Olympus will not tolerate Titanism; Titans belong in the underworld. It is ironic that Titanic's sister ship was named the Olympic, and, in spite of an almost identical build, sailed steadily past her sibling's fate without infamy. When these ships were named, someone failed to take their mythology seriously; the place of the Titan is in Tartaros, a dark prison beneath the sea, as far below the earth's surface as the sky is above. What's in a name? Indeed.

These reflections on naming align with the events and atmosphere surrounding the giant ship herself. Hubris lived not only in title but in the ship's birth into the world and the attitudes which accompanied her maiden voyage. It is well known that Titanic was declared "unsinkable" by elements of the press before she sailed, a claim desperately returned to by the White Star Line in New York once the reports of her distress were known. The claim was due to a special design dividing the bowels of the ship onto several watertight compartments. Yet, when the fateful moment arrived, this innovation was no obstacle for the perfectly positioned jaws of Poseidon, eager to correct the slight of an irreverent age. The iceberg tore into the hull and soon the invading sea flowed over the top of the bulkhead dividers. A side-glance from the deep's protrusions and it was all but over.

Several facts are stunning in their fidelity to the mythopoesis of the tragedy: Titanic's radio room received iceberg warnings several times from other ships. Most were ignored or were not communicated to the bridge. On the bridge warnings were not heeded. Due caution was never observed. True to her name, the Titanic steamed on at a speed, fueled by an unofficial attempt on the Atlantic crossing record. When she set out on her maiden voyage, her stopping capacity and turning ability had never been fully tested during sea-trials. The ship was unwieldy in its bulk and displacement dynamics. She narrowly avoided collision leaving harbor when a smaller ship was sucked into her path. The Titanic carried lifeboats for roughly one-third of the passengers; there was a tendency to think of the ship herself as a lifeboat. Topping off this archetypal congruence a recent discovery suggests that Titanic's hull was constructed of extremely brittle, highly sulfurous steel (Gannon, 1995). This metallurgical matter provides an apt metaphor for the rigid mentality of the whole exercise. Let the alchemists muse upon the corrupting attributes of excess sulfur!

Fate conspired around this combination of irresponsibility, virginal temptation, arrogance, and sheer poetic consistency. The sea was visited by an eerie calm that night so that the lookout did not have the foamy meeting of sea and iceberg to warn him. There was no moonlight to offset the dark of the evening. And had the ship not attempted to maneuver at the last moment, the iceberg would not have punctured as many compartments; most likely she would not have sunk.

When the stern rose high enough into the night, the ship's innards tore loose and roared towards the bow. Her back broke when she settled. As if the Titaness had always known her fate, the ship was taken by the sea with barely a ripple. A few survivors simply stepped off her deck as she headed down. When the screams ceased, the lifeboats drifted into a deathly silence.

The consistency of these themes is crystallized in a 1996 obituary of a Titanic passenger, Miss Eva Hart. The obituary notes that seven of the eight passengers who are still alive today were then too young to remember the event. The remaining survivor, "nearing her 100th birthday, no longer remembers" (Thomas, 1996, 15). Thus, Miss Hart was the "last link of living memory" to the disaster. The article recognizes that no other shipwreck "claimed such a chilling grip on the popular imagination," and that this was "mainly because of a well-publicized exercise in hubris." Nevertheless, it is the recounted words and actions of Miss Hart's mother that are most striking. The claim that the ship was unsinkable

> ...caused Miss Hart's mother such apprehension that even as they walked up the gangplank, her daughter later recalled, she renewed her warning that calling a ship unsinkable was "flying in the face of God." She was so convinced of impending doom, her daughter later maintained, that she slept during the day and stayed awake in her cabin at night fully dressed. (Thomas, 15)

Eva Hart and her mother survived. Eva's father went down with the ship.

This "last living memory" asks to be integrated into our understanding of the catastrophe. Eva Hart's mother perceived an overstepping of cosmic and psychological boundaries; she knew, intuitively, that something had been pushed beyond its limit. She expected a backlash. Such a sensibility, which keeps one eye on the invisible constants of life, is missing from our age. The Titanic disaster carried within it the failed recognition of such invisibles. Tragedy struck hard because, in identifying with Titanism, backs were turned on the Gods, the Furies, and the Fates.

The Titanic may have been less prone to disaster were the atmosphere of hubris confined to the ship itself. We do, after all, get away with a great deal of "flying in the face of God." However, Titanic's hubris reached beyond itself and played too neatly into the hands of a cultural *zeitgeist*. The doomed ship exemplified too perfectly the overly focused technological faith of an entire age. She carried many wealthy exemplars of a cultural revolution based on the philosophies of the Enlightenment, and, in the sometimes impersonal world of archetypal justice, these high-flying industrial elite were prime candidates for corrective descent. At that time, with declarations abounding of science being on the brink of unraveling all mysteries, nothing seemed to stand in the way of progress. No previous age had dispensed so efficiently with ties of religion and nature. But as rationalism was evicting soul's inhabitants, one can hear the voices of dismissed gods inciting Poseidon's act of revenge.

Since that time, we have lost a great deal of the mechanical uncertainty with which the universe was then regarded. Yet we are not so far from the underlying confidence and faith in our own devices. In looking back upon these events, we realize that a significant hubris is still afloat in the culture.

When perceived psychologically, the Titanic confronts our present-day hubris and challenges the dominant Western cultural ethos of "where there's a will there's a way." Recognition of this theme is unnerving. It entails seeing through our fascination with disaster into our state of archetypal possession—our identification with the ways of the Titan. It involves an acknowledgment of our participation in a dream, a story with its own autonomous presence. It fosters a sense of this archetypal movement, placing us within the same tragedy now, today, knowing the way in which we are still aboard a sinking ship. This recognition understands that to forget these things is to sail blindly into a stream of catastrophes, unconsciously provoking recreations of the Titanic tragedy. A psychological perception of Titanic's murmuring

compels a recognition of our Titan roots, an awareness of where
our souls are stirred by the unfinished business and attitudes of
our immediate ancestors. We thereby return our Titanic dreaming
to the dream of the Titan. Then the grip of the giant is felt as an
active myth—a myth that cradles our desire to plow across the
surface of the world and simultaneously underscores the call of
the depths below.

Between Abandon and Binding: The Trouble with Prometheus

Approaching the psychological impact of the Titanic via the
Titan myth leads us to a more specific mythic narrative.
Seeing into the grip of the Titanic story and its archetypal complexity suggests the palpable presence of Prometheus; the Titanic
carried the imprint of this most celebrated Titan more than any
other. Prometheus brings the gifts of ingenuity and invention,
steals fire from Zeus, is bound to Caucasus and has his liver eaten
by day and restored at night, cheats in sacrificial ritual, and is the
divine patron of the human reach beyond the gods. This champion
of human freedom and creativity deserves to be celebrated for
freeing us from a kind of unconscious slavery to the gods. Yet
this freedom comes at a cost.

This Titan's foundational role in humanity's cosmic predicament
is witnessed by Karl Kerényi's subtitle to his work on
Prometheus—"archetypal image of human existence." Bearing a
name that means "forethought," Prometheus is present in any
innovative design which furthers human intentions. He is thus
enmeshed in the dominant cultural ethos of the 19th and 20th
centuries—expanding consciousness, growing industry, technological breakthrough. Prometheus provides the impetus for
scientific discovery and application in the modern world and is most
present whenever these innovations begin to exhibit a godlike power.
And so this particular Titan has also gotten us into some big trouble.
Embracing this Titan we are called to remember the subtitle of Mary
Shelley's *Frankenstein: The Modern Prometheus* and to locate the
monster lurking in the shadow of the Enlightenment's brightness.

The problem with our embrace of Promethean gifts and the freedoms of the enlightened age is that we split off the darker portion of this mythic narrative, namely the tortuous results of untethered innovation. We forget that Promethean abandon can lead to an incarnation of gigantism, which then calls forth a corresponding binding—a chaining to the laws of Zeus. Through this familial association, the unruly behavior of Prometheus' relatives endures and enters the world cloaked in the garb of progress. Blinded by the wonder of his creative gifts, this residue of Titanic ancestry easily escapes our perception. But it is losing sight of the Titan in Prometheus that we become most prone to hubristic excess and its results.

Akin to the sinking of the unsinkable and the tragic demise of celebrated social figures, the myth of Prometheus is one of enantiodromia, of reversal, the assertion of opposites— the revenge of gods whom we fail to recognize when we become enchanted with our own craftiness and power. Here we find out just how much we are tethered to an archetypal psyche. What sailed with Titanic on her maiden voyage were the Promethean dreams of a culture reveling in a perceived emancipation from "superstition" and in an unprecedented industrial reduction of nature to resource. It was through this mythic identification with one side of the Promethean narrative that a ticket on the Titanic became an invitation for catastrophic reversal.

Today we are still poised on the edge of Promethean enantiodromia. And as we approach the 21st century, glued to the information superhighway, technology at our fingertips, our consciousness still identifies with this Promethean forward thinking while remaining largely unconscious of its Titanic background. There is a part of our psyche cruising unawares through dangerous waters, with unchecked speed and techno-faith, focused on the distant horizon of the New World, its back to the Old World. We are still on the deck of the Titanic. And under the belly of the ship, Poseidon and Tartaros await. Irreverent of the depths below with its gods and ancestors, this Titanic tendency accompanies us into postmodernity.

To be Promethean is to enter a Titanic family system and to be situated within the interplay of abandon and binding. Signal the engine room. Ahead slow. These waters need a closer eye.

Promethean Slight and Sacrifice

Prometheus is, like Hermes, a communicator, moving between the divine and human realms. After the Olympic-Titan war, he manages to align himself with Zeus. He is taught mathematics, medicine, astronomy, and architecture by Athena, before educating humanity. When Zeus becomes wary of the increase in human power, it is Prometheus who intervenes on mortals' behalf. However, the relationship unravels when Prometheus cheats in a sacrificial ritual designed to stabilize god-human relations. In this act of cheating, his Titan ancestry shows through. Zeus consequently withholds the gift of fire, which Prometheus promptly steals. The guardian of human ingenuity is punished for his theft, eternally (or nearly so) bound to a cliff-face where an eagle from Zeus picks daily at his liver. The slighted sacrifice sets these events in motion.

This narrative is imbued with insights into our Promethean heritage. Here human-divine tensions coil around a specific limitation: Zeus tolerates human innovation and power by only a marginal degree. At the core of this tension, defining turns and outcomes, lies the ritual sacrifice. Sacrifice—making sacred, surrendering to the presence of a god, humbling oneself to the scheme of things—plays a pivotal role in all myth by determining the mood of archetypal forms which rise to meet the protagonist. Successful sacrifice occasions the recognition of divinity and quiets shadowy beings. Failed sacrifice fuels tragedy. In such a way sacrifice functions as the conduit to the gods par excellence. For Prometheus, sacrifice fails, the divinities are not properly recognized, and both he and his human devotees are drawn into a resultant tragedy which, by divine design, will forever tempt the innovator's soul.

Failing to honor the gods through a sacrifice which would alleviate their distrust of human power sets up the second, darker half of the Promethean narrative. This second movement constitutes the shadow of our preoccupation with human design and fills out the underbelly of the Titanic saga. The exercise of human will can only be tolerated when accompanied by a successful sacrificial recognition of the gods. In the absence of such sacrificial gesture, sacrifice is extracted at greater cost. Sacrifice is imposed. And thus we must beware: Giantism, Titanism, hubris do not sacrifice, but they do invite a sacrificial enantiodromia, a reversal which pulls the whole project down. Sacrifice is then carried out upon us with high tragedy; Hindenburg, Challenger, Chernobyl as witnesses.

In the failure to sacrifice, we are sacrificed.

From these mythic patterns we may distill the following: In so far as the modern-postmodern era identifies itself with Promethean exploits, it must keep its eye on its Titanic roots. To learn this lesson is, I believe, the key to a successful embrace of the technological age. We do not have to dispense with technology, but we must understand its archetypal grounds. Even then, we should expect no more than marginal ascension from Olympus.

Fortunately Prometheus' failed sacrifice and cliff-face binding is not the end of a saga. Two ensuing themes provide us with means for negotiating the Titan's fate, offering a way to mitigate the enantiodromia of the narrative, and thereby opening a path of awareness through our Titanic dream. Both themes concern the restoration of sacrificial attitude.

The myth informs us that Prometheus' "eternal" punishment is temporarily assuaged each night when his shredded liver is restored. This healing quality of the night points to the restorative possibilities in embracing the dark, the underworld of shadow and dream, the counterpart of the bright focused gaze of rational consciousness. Both the chains and the night recall the fate of Prometheus' forbears in the dark prison of Tartaros. This motif thus provides a metaphor for working with unconscious themes (as we have been doing) and for developing a night-vision which perceives depth. Another motif specifies this suggestion by the myth. Prometheus is eventually unbound, freed once again by Zeus. This unbound Prometheus is a different Titan. His ancestry has been worked over, softened, torn up, and refigured. Thus tempered by endless suffering and grief, he agrees to use his foresight to aid Zeus. In this way the Titan returns his gifts to Olympus, sacrificing his own will to that of Zeus, prefiguring the restoration of a sacrificial consciousness we are called to embrace today. Karl Kerenyi writes, "the unbound Prometheus...thenceforth wore a special wreath as a sign of his subjection to the power of Zeus. As another emblem he bore an iron ring, which was said to have had a stone in it to remind him of the crag on which he suffered" (1951, 221-22). These motifs signal the completion of the Promethean narrative. The Titan turns to serve Zeus, fulfilling the punishment of bondage, redeeming his sacrificial failure, and integrating the healing experience of night.

Such images of Promethean restoration guide us through our collective identification with this mythic figure, prime our awareness of the shadow he casts, and offer a way to behold our Titanic dream. Acknowledging the punishment and failure which comes with the narrative, we reunite our Promethean preoccupations with their shadow elements. Noting the context of Prometheus' final redemption, we discover the cosmic demand for a sacrificial attitude. The Titanism which found its enactment in the Titanic disaster, having entered the culture through Promethean abandon, is returned to its ancestry and psychologically grounded within its full mythic narrative. Innovation, invention and freedom also invites bondage; in between lies a sacrificial attitude, lost and regained, and a reverence for what lies beyond us in the dark of the deep.

Lost Sea Wariness

The insights into the collective psyche provided by these mythic themes usher us into a reassessment of the Titanic's fate. If we remain faithful to the details, this disaster, now present to us as an image of unreflected modern-postmodern exploits, can be attributed to the ship's officers and crew who failed to heed iceberg warnings. Think of these figures as the point-men of the cultural complex. Similarly, the extent of the disaster can be traced to the blind arrogance of the ship's designers and owners, and to other crew who, in a state of denial, sent some of the lifeboats off half empty. Even after it was clear that the ship would sink, officers and crew continued to act otherwise. Significant in themselves as points of reflection, these events extend the metaphor of the Promethean shadow and detail the issue of unchecked hubris. They also lead us back to an understanding of that which guards against the perils of Titanism. Were all involved with the Titanic to have maintained their sea wariness, with one eye trained on autonomous powers beyond their control, the disaster would have been avoided. Such sea wariness is the rudimentary matter of the sacrificial attitude I refer to above, for to make sacrifice is to be in awe, to be unsettled and uncertain, ever ready to alter course.

Blind faith in human innovation made otherwise well experienced seamen lose their better judgement. The newness, the power, the size, the spectacle, the sophistication, the elegance, the dreamy wonder of it all closed off all portals to less heady sensibilities. In particular, perhaps the first to go was the capacity to intuit something amiss, a sailor's sixth sense—a sniff, a wind-shift, an omen—the kind of capacity that did not elude Eva Hart's mother. The wonders of science and technology, along with their rational methods, tend to close off these other senses. This is ultimately ironic; the best scientific discoveries are rarely divorced from a playful, intuitive perspective. Many breakthroughs in science come through sudden leaps of intuition. Yet as our world view becomes more mechanistic and less defined by psychic realities, more deterministic and less synchronistic, we lose touch with our soul methodologies. Without these vertical pathways with their visceral connections to the deep, anything crossing the sea of life becomes vulnerable. The stakes are raised when the vessel is Titanic in nature, when the Titanism of the Promethean venture overshadows everything else.

A recovered sea wariness would heed the laws of the sea. Psychologically, it would prioritize the patterns of the psyche. Mythically, it would embrace the wreath of Zeus and the ring which reminds one of punishment and bondage whenever one enters the Promethean realm. Adding verticality attends to all of these modes of perception. Slowing down the big ship, we would reflect, turning ourselves to the past as well as the future, the Old World and the New. In so doing, we would reconfigure the archetypal family, remembering Prometheus' brother. Epimetheus, whose name means "afterthought." We would watch and listen for signs to be intuitively perceived. Journeying into the future on moonless nights requires a moonlit vision, a soft and peripherally sensitive eye. These sensibilities remind us of other presences, and provide us with ears and eyes for the invisibles when we are passing through calm, deep waters. So begins a sacrificial attitude.

James Hersh notes that in Prometheus' punishment he is situated "within a pattern of movement. His manic, nonstop creativity (our science) is forced to rest, to be positioned within a schema, but it is not destroyed. Prometheus' activity has been moved from flux to rhythm" (1982, 156). The Titan's wound and punishment is also an opportunity for attunement to the gods. Conscious suffering is also a meditation on bondage, a lesson on how we are tied to archetypal reality. Turning to this part of the narrative reveals the value of its shadowy element. To digest the complete Promethean narrative is also to find faculties for successful negotiation of the technological age and to disarm Titanic giantism.

These moves against Titanic inflation are all concerned with a turn to the dark, beginning involuntarily through the revenge of the gods, then leading to an acceptance through endurance and sacrifice. When connected to such themes, the Titanic's demise corrects the sun-drenched logos of modern technological vision and moves us into the less defined, less focused, less mechanical world of mythos. A Titan chained on Caucasus or imprisoned in Tartaros is a counterweight for manic modernity.

This awareness makes possible another reading of the Titanic's story, namely that its literal descent to the dark sea bed occurred through the failure of other kinds of descent. And so, if we are still aboard the Titanic by way of our incomplete Promethean lives, still caught in the middle of the narrative, we remain faced with options of descent. James Hillman underlines this very situation after noting the same, "We're aboard the Titanic." He writes:

What is the right action? What do you do while the ship goes down? Strike up the band? Take to the lifeboats? But there's no other shore. Check it with your analyst? Go down like Lord Jim, with honor, courage, decency? At least keep things ship-shape? Or, perhaps, perform the rituals of sinking. (1995, 36).

Hillman makes the correct cultural diagnosis, "The wrath of the immortals against hubris" (36), then suggests a solution which enters the murky depths at the end of the Titanic's journey. "Let there be dark!" (37). Through psychological salvage, the Titanic returns a crucial element of psychological life, specifically, our relation to the unseen, to all below-the-surface phenomena, and prescribes a remedy for sailors overly entranced by the spell of modernity. Which way down? Only sacrifice to the deep keeps the culture afloat.

Insofar as this perspective on descent pertains to the actual ship, we have already failed miserably. Although some survivors and relatives of the disaster's victims have protested the "grave desecration" that salvage of the wreckage entails, few dare think that the Titanic has found her rightful resting place. In the poesis of the soul she headed in the right direction—toward the under-world. By contrast, the compulsion to bring pieces of the ship and her belongings to the surface speaks to a lacking vision of Promethean bondage and an enduring drive to conquer the dark. The popular fantasy of raising the Titanic and the realized efforts to recover her parts reflect the continuing growth of an untetherd technology which asserts itself with ever increasing autonomy.

On the other side of such technical logos the mythic form of events surrounding the Titanic emerge. For most of this century, the Titanic avoided her mapping. Now large chunks of her hull do not want to surface. Expected treasures opened on world-wide television turn out to be less revealing than anticipated. Literal salvage is thwarted. Psychological salvage locates fragments of a myth held in place by an unrecognized Promethean narrative. In this story, the Titanic belongs at the bottom of the ocean—close to her ancestors. This is her fate, a kinship with archetypal principles. And with fifteen hundred lives lost, this kinship is not something to be taken lightly. Here, as myth reveals human lives caught in a larger-than-life archetypal drama, tragedy is returned to its transpersonal origins.

Remembrance and Re-membering

If the archetypal drama of the Titanic disaster remains unrecognized, if the events surrounding her voyage are not remembered, then its basic themes are certain to find more vivid repetition in the 21st century. The culture's engagement with Titanism is far from over.

The story persists that the Titanic sank with the band playing, and the remaining passengers singing "Nearer My God to Thee." For a venture that flew in the face of God, what could be more fitting? Like the dying person wishing to revisit past transgressions, the spontaneous song completes the hubristic neglect of divinities. Beyond themselves, perhaps, these passengers were singing last rites for a sinking giant. It was the distance from god(s) which provoked the disaster, and the movement nearer to the gods in this final, tragic, sacrificial scene. Embracing this very movement would not only be in accord with the dying perspective of the Titanic's passengers, it would also move our fixation on the process of autopsy to the remebrance of a funereal rite. "Nearer my God to Thee" is the soul's response to an event which demonstrated the separation of human endeavor and archetypal integrity. The Titanic's pieces need to be collected in the soul, not in the museum.

References

Broad, W. "Effort to raise part of the Titanic falters as sea keeps history." *The New York Times*. A6, August 31, 1996.

Gannon, R. "The Titanic's Final Secret." *Popular Science*, Feb. 1995.

Hersh, James. "Model-making and the Promethean Ego." *Spring, 1982*: 151-164.

Hillman. James. Untitled Article. *UTNE Reader*. July-August, 1995. 36-37.

Jung, C. G. *Yoga and the West, CW*. London: Kegan Paul and Routledge, 1958.

Kerényi, Karl. *Prometheus: Archetypal Image of Human Existence*. New York: Pantheon, 1963.

Thomas, R. "Eva Hart 91, a last survivor with a memory of Titanic, dies." *The New York Times*, A15, 1996.

ANAÏS NIN AND AMERICAN INVENTION

C. L. SEBRELL

One afternoon in 1962, Anaïs Nin, Barbara Meyerhoff, Deena Metzger, and Carlos Castaneda were having lunch in Southern California. The meeting was at Nin's house, where she lived with Rupert, one of the two husbands she kept simultaneously until the end of her life. The meeting was arranged by Meyerhoff, a co-student of Castaneda's and a fan of his Master's thesis, called *The Teachings of Don Juan*. Castaneda had been threatening to destroy the work because it had gone no farther than the piles of other unsolicited manuscripts at the University of California Press. Meyerhoff convinced him that he should let her handle its publication.

Meyerhoff decided that the best person to be Castaneda's advocate was Anaïs Nin. The luncheon was arranged to introduce the two writers and to convince Nin to read the manuscript. Anaïs was impressed with the book and took it with her to New York, where she promoted it. This was evidently the signal to the University of California Press that what they had in their possession was a work worth publishing. Within weeks Castaneda received

C. L. Sebrell, M.A., is a writer for the *Southbridge Evening News* in Southbridge, Massachusetts. This paper was delivered in August, 1997, at the Myth and Theatre Festival at La Chartreuse, Villeneuve-lez-Avignon, France.

confirmation that *The Teachings of Don Juan* was to be published. Anaïs Nin was pleased with herself and considered it her most successful sponsorship.

Within ten years Castaneda had received not only a Master's Degree but also a Doctorate for his writings, which he insisted were non-fiction. *The Teachings of Don Juan*, and the three books that followed, opened doors to a generation of young people hungry for mystical drug experimentation and for a guru to lead them through it. The books were top sellers and have not been out of print since. Yet definitive work has recently come out[1] showing that Castaneda's writings were completely fabricated or pulled from already published resource books. An entire culture had been tricked by Castaneda's shaman, Don Juan.

It is not as odd as it may seem that the person who first recognized something of value in what Castaneda called "field notes" was Anaïs Nin. Nin was uneducated in and unconnected to the field of anthropology yet immediately recognized the qualities of Castaneda's work. The question is, "Which qualities?"

"Perhaps it takes a writer of fiction to intuit the work of a fellow artist," says Joyce Carol Oates in her 1974 article which was the first to challenge the authenticity of Castaneda's work. "Everyone writes fiction to some extent," she goes on to say, "but most write it without the slightest idea that they are doing so." I think Nin was aware she was writing fictions. Yet, she was not so literal-minded as to not understand that writing what we call "real life" can be a metaphor for the "real life" of the interior world.

Nin's Diaries

Controversy swirls around Nin's diaries in much the same way as it does around Carlos Castaneda's writings of Don Juan. A new book about, or by, Anaïs Nin comes out at least every two years. The newest is a book called *Recollections of Anaïs Nin*, a collection of essays by her contemporaries. Edited by Benjamin Franklin V, *Recollections of Anaïs Nin*, introduces fifteen of Nin's contemporaries who loved her, hated her, or were simply confused by her.[2]

Franklin wrote in the introduction to his book that he wanted to give Anaïs the attention he felt she deserved but has never fully received. This is not Franklin's first attempt to pay homage to the woman that influenced him as a graduate student, and many introductions to the numerous books about her, or by her, begin with a similar complaint. This in fact was Nin's own endless complaint during her life. She never felt she was given her literary due.[3] Yet it is possible that this complaining is part of her balancing act, similar to the one she performed to successfully maintain two husbands simultaneously on opposites coasts of the United States. It leaves us guessing as to just which side of the bar she will fall. Is her diary fact or is it fiction?

Nin's life continues to fascinate readers. Deirdre Bair's biography of Nin, which won the American National Book Award in 1995, is almost six hundred pages of detail about the multiplicity and complexity of Anaïs Nin. She manipulated, lied, stole, seduced, bragged, and betrayed. We see for the first time just how Nin invented herself. Nin did not enact everything "bad" about women so much as she expressed the darker side of the feminine unconscious.

I think Nin embodied all the things about women that we try to repress. She plunged full force into the unconscious and acted out what psychoanalysis had told us all along we have wanted to do but could not, even sleeping with her father as a mature woman. The beautiful woman of so many faces, who "literally" experienced all of women's undisclosed fantasies became a monster.

But the nature of monsters *is* multiplicity, and to deny women their monsters, as feminism often does, is to deny them their humanity. It is a subtle injustice. The standard set upon women to be infallible mothers, energetic and compassionate wives or lesbians, morally incorruptible members of the community, as well as successful and obedient employees, leaves us inhuman. There is no room for murderous feelings, fatigue, frustration, or an inner and relentless demand for attention. In Anaïs Nin we find a woman who lived out "shadow," which can partly be defined as the ugly unconscious that we hide from the world around us.

Writing about Nin

It is no surprise that Nin had her enemies. Anatole Broyard, a well known American essayist and critic writing in New York in the fifties and sixties (who is a featured essayist in *Recollecting Anais Nin*), finds Anaïs a difficult and manipulative woman. In one of his well-known essays, Broyard describes her, nearing the end of her life, as a statue. He met her at her home, and describes their meeting from the perspective of a young man encountering for the first time the famous Anaïs.

> Anaïs was a medium-sized woman with a very pale face, like a Japanese actress. She was classical looking, in the sense of a form that has become rigidified. Her hair was dark, straight, parted in the middle and pulled back. Her lipstick was precise, her eyebrows shaved off and penciled in, giving the impression that she had written her own face....(*Recollecting Anaïs Nin*, 19)

Certainly she was aware of every move and action in her life that would contribute to her image, the character that she created to live the life of a diary which was then to be published as her "work." Broyard goes on to say:

> Anaïs was like someone at a party, dancing, drinking and batting her eyes...Anaïs was unconscious of the picture she made . . . [she] had already posed for her statue. She had posed for it without knowing where it would be put up.

Deena Metzger, a writer and lecturer in Los Angeles (and another essayist in *Recollections of Anaïs Nin*), remembers a different Anaïs. Metzger finds her confused and frustrated by her contemporaries' desire to make a sculpture of her: "I came into [Nin's] house and saw that she was upset. 'I am not a paragon,' Nin cried out. 'I will not be set on a pedestal.'"

Metzger decided, ironically, when one considers how constructed Nin's life was, to relate to her as a person rather than a caricature or a literary figure, a resolution that Broyard never made. Of course we love to read Broyard's thinly disguised dislike for a formidable and sexual woman. However, the New York scene in which many new writers are often given reputations they do not necessarily deserve was crushing for Anaïs. The fantasy of "purity" of art form and "genuineness" of talent went against a woman who had completely invented her life.

But it was the feminists (including Metzger) who put her up on the pedestal she disliked, a place where it is unlikely that any human could live a life. The new, aggressive femininsm of the sixties and seventies left Nin dazed. Many of the ideals of feminism left no room for the shadowy side of women, the side that Anaïs Nin lived to explore. It is no wonder she was not happy with her newfound stature.

Any careful reader today can spot the art and artifice in Nin's work. We are fooled at first because much of her work is presented as diaries, the one place where many people keep the most cherished and ugly secrets about themselves. It is clear from day one that Nin fully intended to have her diaries read, a notion that would horrify many people. One might say that Anaïs Nin and her lover, Henry Miller, frequently wrote about the same things, but that Nin presented hers as non-fiction whereas Miller did not. As a result we are less offended by and less suspicious of Miller's writing. We derive pleasure from trying to discover what is auto-biographical about Miller's books but constantly pick Nin's apart to discover what is fictional about them. Perhaps this is one reason why Miller's writings were more readily accepted than Nin's right from the start.

Castaneda, Nin, and "Truth"

Carlos Castaneda avoided a situation such as Nin's at first by presenting his work as "field notes" done as research for his Master's thesis. He was protected by the thick walls of academia as well as his own foresight in keeping his biographical information a mystery. To this day Castaneda has either withheld the facts of his life or has given contradictory information about it. His birthdate is unknown and aspects of his life are unverifiable, such as his supposed military service. In much the same way that Don Juan's existence is unreal, so is Castaneda's. With the acceptance of Don Juan as fact, the Nin-esque invention of the Doctor of Anthropology who had access to extraordinary experiences was complete.

Some people within the men's movement have rasied Castaneda up to idol status because of his exploration into the male consciousness. Surprisingly, the poet Robert Bly, who became a leader of the men's movement, was one of Castaneda's earliest and harshest critics. Bly saw in Castaneda's writings not a truth but a well-told myth. Perhaps the reason why Castaneda's work was so powerful for so many was that it did tell a myth, a story with such universal appeal that it would immediately be picked up by readers hungry for a guru to lead them through their experiments in self-discovery with psychoactive drugs.

Just as Broyard tried to dispel Nin's invented persona by publicly refuting the truth of the diaries, Bly refuted the possibility that Castaneda was telling the truth about Don Juan. Bly did this by arguing that Castaneda's motives were all wrong. Bly writes, "Castaneda good-naturedly gives the capitalist college student what they want—fantasies of gaining power without becoming more compassionate or more honest." Bly uses Freudian diagnostic weapons to accuse Castaneda of being stuck in an "anal stage" because the book is obviously devoid of genuine sexuality with women. "Naturally this shows in content, where no one ever goes off behind the bushes without being noticed." In Bly's eyes Castaneda's crime was to regress into showing men and women in the "joyful genital stage" while narrating it all in the language of the "anal stage." Bly was unable to see that Castaneda was already post-Freudian.

Anatole Broyard and Robert Bly were right in that they sensed an "untruth," and this untruthfulness is what was so offensive to them. Yet what both of them failed to see was the incredible skill it takes to invent oneself, to create and write a life as fascinating as Nin's and Castaneda's. Broyard and Bly responded with the characteristic cry, "You can't fool me!"

It seems that Nin and Castaneda committed a crime against such assumptions. Tolstoy, Faulkner, Dickens, and Hardy were all writing "fictions," yet at the same time were giving us "biography" and "history" as truth. The idea that these were "novels" does not make them any less "true." We have little problem accepting as "true" what is presented as "fiction." The problem enters when what is "fictional" is presented to us as "truth." This is what is seen as the ultimate breach of a reader's trust.

In archetypal psychology it is often said that any truth is fictional. Any story a person tells must come from a perspective filled with prejudices and notions that will effect the "truth" of the story. With biographies, especially autobiographies, this phenomenon is made more clear. Janet Malcolm attempted to write a "truthful" biography of Sylvia Plath, the poet who committed suicide in part to spite her husband, the poet Ted Hughes. Malcolm found the task impossible. She writes:

> We must always take the novelist's and the playwright's and the poet's word, just as we are almost always free to doubt the biographer's or the autobiographer's or the historian's or the journalist's. In imaginative literature we are constrained from considering alternative scenarios— there are none. This is the way it *is*. Only in non-fiction does the question of what happened and how people thought and felt remain open. (Malcolm, 138)

It is the readers' right to believe fully in the fictional and question completely the nonfictional. Many readers of biography find pleasure in discovering cracks in the mask.

In attempting a biography of Plath, Malcolm discovered that Plath created her mythic character by killing it. In so doing, she made her character, however unintentionally, forever young and enshrouded in scandal. But although Plath did not have Nin's flair for self-invention, Malcolm discovered that many of Plath's letters (published as factual) are fictions.

Carlos Castaneda made a career of his fictions, just as did Anaïs Nin. Yet the role of facts and truths in both of their works becomes overshadowed by the fictions. Castaneda *did* have mystical experiences, if only in his imagination. No one would be able to write about such experiences if there were not some meaningful, and real, experience behind it. The question perhaps is, "What is an experience?" The mythical truths in Castaneda's works are interior truths, the truths that are not provable, factual or real. Castaneda was trying to get us to see another form of truth.

It is interesting that while Nin and Castaneda were working on their writings, Ernest Hemingway was being forced through electro-shock therapies at the Mayo clinic in Minnesota to rid him of "delusions" that the FBI was following him. The devastating treatments were followed shortly by Hemingway's suicide and then an attack, even abandonment, of his life's work by his colleagues and friends. Hemingway's stories of persecution by the FBI were never even explored as truth, and he was diagnosed as delusional and paranoid. In the public's and his fourth wife's eyes, Hemingway was committing the worst of crimes—he was telling fictions and insisting on their truth. Today we know the FBI *was* after Hemingway, and that he was tortured and destroyed for a crime he never did commit—telling fiction as truth.

Nin and Castaneda considered their life-stories malleable. A biography, they taught us, is a thing which can be shaped and designed to create a persona. Should we be more generous in forgiving Anaïs Nin and Carlos Castaneda for their breach of the reader/writer contract because their non-fictions have had such an enormous impact on our culture? There is little question both writers influenced the way the American mind thinks. The Don Juan books are in large part responsible for the new multiculturalism in America. Don Juan took America by storm and opened up discussion of a "non-Western" form of knowledge. Anaïs Nin helped women to recognize and admit that they, too, have pleasure to gain from sex, an essential liberation. These are important and real, changes in American culture, and what they invented has become a large part of the *reality* of American life and soul today.

Notes

[1]See Ward Churchill's essay, "Carlos Castaneda: The Greatest Hoax Since Piltdown Man," in *Fantasies of a Master Race*, Monroe, Maine: Common Courage Publishers, 1992.

[2]If this is actually an ancestor of Benjamin Franklin, it is ironic he chose to write biography. The autobiography of the historical Franklin is famous for the author claiming he did things it is rather certain he did not do.

[3]There are enough books by or about Anaïs Nin to completely fill three full shelves at the Homer Babbage Library at the Univeristy of Connecticut. Few authors of the twentieth century have been afforded so much attention.

Works Cited

Broyard, Anatole. *Men, Women and Other Anticlimaxes*. New York: Methuen, 1980.

Bryfonski, Dedria and Gerard Seneck, eds. *Contemporary Criticism: Excerpts from Criticism of the Works of Today's Novelists, Poets, Playwrites, and Other Creative Writers*. Vol. 12. Detroit: Book Tower, 1980.

Castaneda, Carlos. *The Teachings of Don Juan*. New York: Simon and Shuster, 1972.

_____. *Journey to Ixtlan*. New York: Simon and Shuster, 1972.

Churchill, Ward. *Fantasies of a Master Race*. Monroe, Maine: Common Courage Publishers, 1992.

Franklin, Benjamin, V. *Recollections of Anais Nin*. Athens, Ohio: Ohio UP, 1996.

Malcom, Janet. "Annals of Biogrpahy: The Silent Woman." *The New Yorker*. August 23 and 30, 1993.

Nasso, Christine, ed. *Contemporary Authors: A Bio-Bibliographical Guide to Current Authors and Their Works*. Vol. 25-28. Detroit: Book Tower, 1977.

Oates, Joyce Carol. "Don Juan's Last Laugh." *Psychology Today*, September, 1974.

No Way!

SHEILA GRIMALDI-CRAIG

Don DeLillo, *Underworld*. Scribner, New York, 1997. Pp. 827. Cloth, $27.50.

I was all set to review Don DeLillo's new novel, *Underworld*, as my enthusiastic contribution to the American Soul issue of *Spring*. DeLillo's paranoid novels have long provided such grimly delicious reading, always intense but in the kind of sickeningly refreshing psychological way I need sometimes when I've seen too many Tom Hanks movies, read too many James Redfield prophecies, or heard one too many Maya Angelouisms. DeLillo has always been closer to the depressing side of life than most anybody writing in America. And he's convincing: like all our really serious writers, from Salinger to Pynchon, DeLillo has hidden from celebrity, genuinely and intelligently afraid of "the media," the public, the professoriat and all. I figured DeLillo's take on the last half century of American life as encapsulated in his big new book would be just the ticket for this issue of *Spring*, that it would be the darkest but most acute read of the year, one that gets American Soul in exactly its right place at this moment. It even says so on the book jacket, "It takes the reader deeply into the lives of Nick

Sheila Grimaldi-Craig taught for many years in the Connecticut public schools. She is the regular reviewer for this journal.

and Klara and into modern memory and the soul of American culture." I should have known better.

The trouble with *Underworld* is that you have to agree to take the whole last half of the twentieth century of American life as one big unremitting waste, nuclear and otherwise, before you start. (The protagonist is in the waste business.) I suppose I should be willing to do that for the sake of a good read—suspend my disbelief in order to receive the chills and spills of great entertainment in return—but in this case, to keep turning the pages you have to be either Forrest Gump or a newly-politicalized sophomore in some 1960s Liberal Arts college that got frozen in time.

"Remarks are not literature, Hemingway," Gertrude Stein is supposed to have told her young protege back in the days when he was submitting his stories to her for criticism and instruction. But in post-modern fiction, remarks are everything. *Underworld* is, unfortunately, that wonder of wonders that all the ideologues clamor for in American Lit courses, the political novel (the kind they strive to write in France). Unfortunately, it is not a soulful or psychological one. The implicit tone of moral scorn, the emotional distancing that DeLillo maintains from the characters and their actions, hardly leads to the kind of engagement that can hold a reader, at least this reader, for such a long undertaking. And if you don't care for the characters somehow except as props and examples of bad American life, if you can't identify with any of them, what are you doing here?

Even in the opening scene, where Frank Sinatra, Jackie Gleason and Toots Shor are sitting together—with J. Edgar Hoover on the aisle—at the legendary 1951 New York Giants / Brooklyn Dodgers baseball game where Bobby Thomson hit a pennant winning home run, you don't read for the potential pleasure of the scene, the pleasure of four classic American characters observing things on a significant day. Rather, you're in for the distastefulness of the gluttonous Gleason's vomiting on the foppish Sinatra's shoes, for the ominousness of Hoover (by now such a stock bad guy in our literature it would be original for him not to be sinister) receiving news of Russian nuclear tests while watching the game, or for the story of what happened to the home run (ho hum) baseball itself, the many hands through which it passed in the ensuing years.

I should have known there was something wrong when media central, *The New York Times Book Review*, started thumping so hard for this one, always a bad sign. Up until recently, "the national newspaper of record," as *The Times* likes to call itself, preferred to dismiss DeLillo as a "cult" author. That was okay with me—I've been into so many of their cults over the years it's almost to the point where if they put someone or something on their cult list, I'm ready to join. From the old-fashioned Catholic Church of my childhood to the newspaper burying Marshall McLuhan of the 60s, from the utterly non-traditional poetry of Charles Olson and the Black Mountain School in the 50s to what those cigar-chomping girls in the back room of *The Times Book Review* currently like to call "the Jung Cult," I think I've been there.

But as a (library) card carrying member of the DeLillo cult, I always found his books to be desperately on target, that is, grim, and far truer reads than the labored sociology tracts of the American Left and Right, another book on Freud, or the latest insufferable Bloomsbury twitter that *The Times Book Review* always wants to sell me.

The last DeLillo I read, *Mao II*, for example, was about a whining J. D. Salinger-like recluse who comes out of hiding for some crazy idealist malarkey about rescuing a young poet from terrorists. It was terrific! The rescue part was a little silly, but the elaborate reclusion of a great writer, telling so much as it did about DeLillo's own delicate paranoid struggle to deal with public life in mass America, was fascinating. And before that there was *Libra*, a novel about pathetic Lee Harvey Oswald and his paranoid struggle with same.

But *Underworld* just doesn't do it for me, and I'm not sure why. The masterful capturing of contemporary speech and dialogue, for which DeLillo has long been credited, is still there, yet it doesn't save 827 pages of what soon becomes a rather tiring form of one-note alienation from American life. *Underworld*, by contrast with DeLillo's earlier books, is just too self-conscious of how the language as currently spoken must be faithfully documented. It works so hard at it that it begins to reflect back on its own best art:

People weren't saying Oh wow anymore. They were saying No way instead and she wondered if there was something she might learn from this.(382)

Not much, one concludes, as we watch the artist Klara struggle with her (needless) post-modern paranoid fears that she might be missing something. She's so alert to her language worry she misses the value of what language describes, which is to say, life itself.

Elmore Leonard, whose crime novels are even better than DeLillo's at getting American speech patterns down, never has this problem—I guess if your world is already utterly criminal and corrupt, you can afford to acknowledge at least once and awhile the surprising grace and richness of being that also peoples those sleazy Miami racetracks, and you know all along that Leonard knows all along that those slimeball, low-life haunts he writes about have value. I mean, that's one place American soul really is, if it's anywhere pinpointable: it's in the ability to recognize the value of dark subjects, it's in the fascination of our dumb alienation itself, it's in our wanting to know more about Frank Sinatra than he deserves.

There's a passage, for example, in Michael Ventura's gritty 1996 novel, *The Death of Frank Sinatra*, that gets right at the soul of Las Vegas, a city that millions of (tasteless) Americans love, and with good (bad) reason:

> Turning right onto Stewart Avenue, he saw how the city sparkled in the valley, each single light precise and strident. The white beam of the Luxor Pyramid shot straight up, and the blue-green of the MGM, the bright red of the Rio, the ice blue of Caesar's, the gold hue of the Mirage, the glare of the strip and the dimmer pulse of downtown, and all the tiny lights of homes that spread into the Mojave, the neon language of his world, said to him and to all in an electric voice that was high-tension indeed: "You can have what you want. You can have what you want. You must have what you want. You must have what you want. What do you want? What do you want? Just say. Just admit. It will be yours." (84)

To my ear, that's closer to what Las Vegas (or America, or God) says, and closer as well to what our attitude should be to Las Vegas (or America, or God). There's paranoia here, and with paranoia there's soul. But there's no politics—please!

DeLillo's gift for paranoia has always been about as perfect as it gets. But that gift, too, I fear, has become part of this big new media-friendly political package:

> He was locked to his chair, mind-locked and gravity-trapped, aware of the nature of the state he was in but unable to think himself out. He was bent to the weight of the room, distrustful of everyone and everything here. Paranoid. Now he knew what it meant, this word that was bandied and bruited so easily, and he sensed the connections being made around him, all the objects and shaped silhouettes and levels of knowledge—not knowledge exactly but insidious intent. But not that either—some deeper meaning that existed solely to keep him from knowing what it was... He knew he wasn't part of some superficial state that people like to borrow from when they say they're feeling paranoid. This was not secondhand. This was real and deep and true. It was all the one-syllable words that mean we aren't kidding. It was also familiar in some strange Paleolithic root-eating way, a thing retained in the snake brain of early experience.
>
> He studied the shoe on the foot of someone seated near him. It was an Earth shoe, one of those functional, sensible, unsexy, shallow-heeled and vaguely Scandinavian items of fad footwear, the shy, androgynous and countercultural shoe, unthreatening to the environment or the species, and he wondered why it looked so sinister. (421-422)

Okay, maybe it's supposed to be funny. I find it a paranoia that ends paranoia. Everybody in this book is so busy being paranoid about something small, they are failing to be paranoid about the supposedly epochal event of the age, the nuclear nightmare. But can failed paranoia, or missed paranoia, or what can only be called "establishment" paranoia, hold the truly paranoid reader (me) for long? The comic appeal of such a state may work for awhile—at least it did in the heyday of those grandaddy postmodern paranoids, Burroughs and Vonnegut, and it sometimes works even with the latest episode of television's endearingly paranoid Dr. Katz. Paranoid America is one funny country; one scary country, too. But real paranoids don't have time for this stuff. If you're just kidding around, DeLillo, count me out.

But why should he be kidding all of a sudden? I know we don't read post-moderns for plot. In DeLillo the plots are not what the stories are about. They're devices to keep unfolding scenes of further paranoid grimness. Thus, in this book our waste management protagonist journeys, in one scene, to the new Russia. He meets with his Russian counterpart in Waste Containment, who explodes plutonium waste under ground for the new world market in such— and is then taken to the Museum of Misshapens, where post-Chernobyl fetuses are displayed. But the effect, gruesome as it is, is just too predictable. It's slick. "Victor is a man who evidently likes to deepen the texture of an experience," we are told. That is what DeLillo's plot moves usually do, too, although here they don't deepen so much as they rub our noses, one more time, in our nuclear history.

The whole thing has about as much punch to it as an editorial in *The New York Times*, with whose views on American life, and how bad things always are, it seems indistinguishably in agreement. The problem with *Underworld* is that it isn't really "Underworld" at all—it doesn't much care about the screams and passions of American soul, or even its Misshapens, for that matter, let alone its rare and singular glories, like Bobby Thomson's home run, only the mutually agreed upon alienation that our official culture itself now tries to promulgate, ironically, for its own self-protection. It's always been a tough sell in this country, but *The Times* seems convinced that alienation, or at least its own watered down and highly saleable version of it, is the smart position to have when your "all that's fit" editorial probities are being ignored every day by the likes of, God-help-us, America Online. So you routinely give the country a big "F" for bad behavior.

The Times, especially its *Book Review*, has always wanted to be the arbiter of American soul, though it's too anti-paranoid to be in such a position. It's too rationalist, too moralist, too liberal to do such a job. Like DeLillo himself, I fear now, it's too successful to be paranoid. It doesn't love the madness enough. It fails the Las Vegas test. It may, today, begrudge a certain fondness to Frank Sinatra, now that he's eighty-two, but you know it's never going to dig Wayne Newton.

With DeLillo's new book, strangely, he sounds like a straight-man, if not quite a pitch-man, for the official New York media barons. For this book he has given abundant interviews, and he's even doing book tours to promote sales. If you know his earlier work, you can imagine how much this must pain him. Imagine Dostoievsky doing book signings at Borders. Maybe he's become *The Spy Who Came In From The Cold* (my kind of Cold War novel), wanting out of the increasingly chilly paranoid trenches where nobody buys your stuff except your cult followers, and wanting into those cozy New York literary clubs (*The Times*, *The New Yorker*, *Harper's*, *The New York Review of Each Others' Books*) where a disdainful moral tone for "the waste culture" out there has a better chance of payoff. Sure enough, there's even a Web site now (www.haas.berkeley.edu/ ~ gardner/delillo.html) called "Don DeLillo's America."

I'm disappointed, because for a long time I regarded him as one of the most interestingly scary people writing today. I guess it's one thing to be the genuinely "alienated" writer he once was, the quiet, Jesuit-trained, hard-nosed Italian kid from the Bronx who could write so sensitively about our national psyche and who possessed one of the most immaculate versions of what Hemingway always said was the most essential thing for a good writer ("a built-in shit detector"); it's quite another to be the toast of the New York Book Establishment for writing an 827 page treatise they can all rally behind. I knew DeLillo was radical, but I thought he was more radical than that.

Our soul is our past, our remembered (and unremembered) past. And America's is funny as well as sad, as well as contemptible and enchanting, ugly, ennobling, and everything else. You have to be vulnerable to it, you have to be willing to fall for it every so often, to do it justice. But to put the comfortable *New York Times* mono-grid over remembering it, that so predictable one-size-fits-all tone of the "radical chic" Establishment's official moral position, is a loss.

As I write this, the editors of *The Sunday Times Book Review* have just put *Underworld* on their Christmas book (!) recommendation list with the comment, "Here bland, hopeful American life glows with the sick light of betrayal...and ambient moral fear pinches everyone."

Forgive me, Klara, but no way!

Serrano Rap

SHEILA GRIMALDI-CRAIG

Miguel Serrano, *C. G. Jung and Hermann Hesse*. Daimon, Einsiedeln, Switzerland, 1997. Pp. 137. Paper. $15.95.

What was Robert Hinshaw, the clever American publisher of Daimon books, thinking of when he decided to republish this 1966 memoir? Was he trying to show us, as if yet more evidence were needed, how obnoxiously self-serving some of the people were who imposed themselves on Jung and Hesse in the last years of their lives? "Thank God I'm Jung and not a Jungian," Jung himself used to say, and here we see why.

Serrano, a wealthy Chilean politician and writer, informs us in a Foreword to the present edition that the original version, called *The Hermetic Circle*, brought many "youthful pilgrims" carrying the book "in their knapsacks" to his door, as they retraced the journey he had made to Hesse's palazzo on Lago Lugano in Switzerland. But they were "retracing" it because Serrano had moved into Hesse's house himself after Hesse died.

In 1951, when Serrano first went there, Hesse had posted a sign outside saying "Please, no visitors." Serrano went through the gate anyway and at the door found another request not to bother the seventy-three year old author, though Serrano says it was too dark out to read the sign at the time:

When a man has reached old age
And has fulfilled his mission,
He has a right to confront
The idea of death in peace.
He has no need of other men;
He knows them and knows enough about them.
What he needs is *peace.*
It isn't good to visit this man or to talk to him,
To make him suffer banalities.
One must give a wide berth
To the door of his house,
As if no one lived there.

Serrano, like most bounders, apparently did not think this sort of thing was meant for people of culture like himself. He had brought along his book of poems as proof to the master of his fellow standing as an author. He entered the house without an invitation, and was met politely by Hesse a few minutes later, who, sure enough, exchanged banalities with the young man. ("You should let yourself be carried away, like the clouds in the sky..." etc. etc.) To make it sound like he has spent hours with Hesse, and to set a mood, Serrano says, "Outside the late afternoon sky began to pale," forgetting that when he barged into the house shortly before he said it was already dusk and too dark to read the warning on the door! But we are supposed to be enchanted with this "first" meeting and feel that the questions Serrano has asked the master are "like those that Siddhartha asked the Buddha."

Damian, Siddhartha, Steppenwolf, The Journey to the East, The Glass Bead Game, though originally known only to a German middle class audience between World Wars I and II, and to almost no one outside Germany even after Hesse was awarded the Nobel Prize for Literature in 1946, are indeed great books. But by 1951, the year Serrano made his first visit, all of Hesse's books were remaindered and out of print in the United States, and most young Germans felt Hesse was the romantic property of their parents' generation, a generation most preferred to forget. Hesse's books became sensational best-sellers only after the American novelist Henry Miller recommended in that same year that *Siddhartha* be translated into English. *Steppenwolf* soon became a Beat Generation bible. Colin Wilson, in *The Outsider,* declared Hesse "the symbolic figure of the age," and in an article called "Hermann Hesse: Poet of the Interior Journey," Timothy Leary brought the psychedelic enlightenment into the fold. It didn't last. Those dreary German novelists, Heinrich Böll and Gunther Grasse, led a Leftist campaign to repudiate Hesse's influence on impressionable kids, and today, here and abroad, his books seem to have been replaced by Nintendo. (For all this and more, see Ralph Freedman's excellent 1978 biography, *Hermann Hesse, Pilgrim of Crisis.*)

Yet Serrano, in his 1991 Foreword, denounces Americans and what they did to the sacred Hesse of his imagination, especially in a movie version of *Steppenwolf,* authorized by Hesse's son Heiner, where, lest anyone got the wrong impression, the protagonist makes several denunciations of Nazism. Serrano's contempt for this is a bit much: "The total lack of discretion and respect shown by the North Americans and the information media, as well as their lack of culture, led them to try to destroy a German—and so German!—author's links with the very roots of his nationality so as to use him for their own aims, to use him in the great conspiracy of 'universal revelation,' so to speak, which had just begun and which was soon to spread with vertiginous speed across the whole planet. This phenomenon was doubtless encouraged by the vast lack of culture which was generalized and propagated by so many circles in the United States of America."

Serrano is not a Nazi, nor was he, during his various Chilean ambassadorships, as far as I know, even a flunky of the infamous General Pinochet. (He claims to have been appointed an ambassador not because of his wealth or family connections but simply because Chile honors its poets.) His *Siddhartha* and *Steppenwolf,* however, are different from the ones that he insists the rest of the world has misread, misled by the "great conspiracy" of those Kultur-less Americans who admired Hesse's gift for "interiority" and "inward journey." Serrano's Hesse, like his Jung, are instead the last hope for re-staging a worldwide Roman Catholic Christianism as the answer to materialism's triumph. Like others who felt their religion threatened by 20th century science and culture, Serrano saw in Hesse (who had been psychoanalyzed by Jung) an argument for a neo-Christian psychology: "The question which the Western Christian now has to face is whether, without losing his individuality, he can accept the coexistence of light and shadow and of God and the devil. To do so, he will have to discover the God who was Christian before the personalized Christ and who can continue in a viable form after him. Such a deity would be the Christ of Atlantis, who once existed publicly, and who still continues to exist—even though submerged under the deep waters of our present civilization." That's his rap.

Much of the book has Serrano telling Hesse (or Jung) his own banal prejudices about Orientals or the people of India, about whom, because of his ambassadorship there, he feels expert: "The idea of the *persona* has not yet reached the Orient, and the personal isn't understood, any more than love is, in the Western Christian sense. That is not a criticism; it is simply a statement of fact."

Hesse and Jung are scrupulously polite at all times, always agreeing to talk to him when he presents himself, and Serrano takes advantage of this to keep coming back. At one point, he says to Hesse: "I wonder whether there is something in the Hermetic Circle [a term Hesse had used to describe everyone interested in the psychology of the self] which suggests that we had all known one another in other lives? Why else have you both been so congenial to me?" Why indeed?

The book is staggering in its author's lack of perception. He seems to have identified with his subjects. After both Jung and Hesse died, in 1961, Serrano tells us of his horror at the thought that he will have to live now in a world of concrete and asphalt.

> In such a world I would be a total alien, unable to find a single niche for myself. But I then realized that people like Hesse and Jung had faced similar difficulties. They had now departed and were now untouched by the mechanization of the earth, and they had achieved other worlds...I myself would now have to make a similar effort...This I had to do if I was to save myself from the leaden desert into which the world was being transformed by machines...It was Sunday, and I

was alone in my house in Belgrade, surrounded by my Oriental paintings and sculptures. I decided that I would celebrate a ritual and listen to the magic music that Hesse had loved, Bach's Mass in B Minor. I lit a few sandalwood sticks and placed the records in the gramophone.

Apparently, gramophones don't count as "machines" when one is immersed in a purist's fantasyland.

Infatuation with Jung by people who met him was by no means uncommon, but rarely has a book of such singular pretentiousness as this been the result. In 1959, Serrano sought out the eighty-five year-old Jung at the Hotel Esplanade in Locarno, where he was vacationing. He waited in the lobby until Jung came down the stairs to dinner, then made his move. Jung invited him to sit down in a corner, where they chatted about India. "I had the feeling that the interview was more like a meeting of old acquaintances than a first encounter. It was like meeting someone who was expecting you, and who you knew was expecting you."

When Jung returned to Zürich immediately after this, Serrano telephoned his house to ask if he could see him again. Jung's secretary, Aniela Jaffé, said no, that Jung "was receiving no visitors" and was not in good health. Such considerations, of course, never stop people like Serrano. "I then told her that I had been with him in Locarno and pleaded with her to ask whether I might come." She put down the phone and came back a few minutes later saying that Dr. Jung would see him that afternoon. The inscription over the door to Jung's house said in Latin, "*Vocatus atque non vocatus, Deus aderit.*" ("Called or not called, God will be present.") The same might have been said of Serrano.

The following year, Serrano wrote a book of stories about the Queen of Sheba, loosely designed to illustrate Jungian ideas about the Collective Unconscious and the Anima. He sent the manuscript to Jung with the message that "you are the only person who can properly understand these pages." Jung sent him a polite one page reply, with the usual gracious comment one sends to an author who sends you his book, in this case calling it "an extraordinary piece of work," and "highly poetic." Serrano, never one to miss an opportunity, however, then writes to Jung to ask if he could use the letter as a preface, not telling us of course that it is precisely because of "Jung's Preface" that the book, otherwise undistinguished, would get published by a major New York publisher. In a chapter that Serrano has the colossal *chutzpah* to call "Dr. Jung Writes A Preface For My Book," he says of Jung's two paragraphs, "This then, is the story of Dr. Jung's collaboration with me in a symbolic and poetical work. I don't believe that in all his long life he wrote another Preface for a purely literary work."

Serrano did finally elicit a letter of some substance from Jung, one of his last, in which Jung warns, "When, for instance, the belief in the god Wotan vanished and nobody thought of him anymore, the phenomenon originally called Wotan remained; nothing changed but its name, as National Socialism has demonstrated on a grand scale." It is unfortunate that we have to wade through pages and pages of Serrano's own windy letters first, however, before we get to Jung's.

One day, long after Jung died, Serrano took his son to see Jung's house in Küsnacht. Jung's grandson answered the door but had the good sense to refuse to let Serrano, whom he didn't know, come in to show his young son "around." Only when Jung's daughter arrived by chance and the situation was explained, was our author admitted. "It sounds odd," he says, his intrusive sense of mission still burning as ever to the end, "but I really believe that Jung was once again receiving me at his house; he was incapable of letting me stand at the door like a stranger."

An Exchange of Letters Between
Sheila Grimaldi-Craig and Sonu Shamdasani

Dear Sonu Shamdasani,

As the regular book reviewer for *Spring Journal*, I have received several suggestions in the past few weeks from our readers to review Richard Noll's latest book, *The Aryan Christ*. I have not read the book, and, frankly, I did not intend to. Having read and reviewed his previous book, *The Jung Cult*, it seemed to me that he must be on some kind of crusade against Jung and Jungians, and so, enough already.

I did, however, read the outrageous review of *The Aryan Christ* in *The New York Times Book Review*, and it has almost succeeded in making me sympathize with Richard Noll! *The New York Times* has, for many years, of course taken the position that Freud and Freudians are the proper psychology and readership of their newspaper. Freud will keep New Yorkers sane, it is believed, and committed to the clichés and shibboleths upon which so much of "literary" New York (what dreamers!) bases its product. To this end, they routinely get these same two English professors (Walter Kendrick from Fordham and Perry Meisel from Columbia, who together wrote a book about Freud's English translators), to review books on Jung or Jungians. It's always the same predictable ideological buncomb—these two guys must not be able to stand the fact that nobody reads or buys their own boring sludge and so they keep scoring Department points (it adds up to what are called "merit raises") by doing hack reviews for *The Times*.

Kendrick's most recent dismissal of Jung ("annoying to have around but dangerous only to those whose stupidity deserves what it gets") says of Noll's *Aryan Christ* that it "fails to convince me that any serious damage has been done by a few people's adherence to an obviously wacko creed." The arrogance and hauteur of this kind of "reviewing" would not bother me at all—anybody who's ever been to an Ivy League college, or even Kendrick's own Jesuit factory, knows what to do with English professors' baloney—except that it means in this case that Noll's book, whatever it has to say, is relegated to the same sanctimonious trash-pile that so many other books are that diverge from the approved reading list. (I am always amazed, for example how the books of one of my favorite authors, May Sarton, over her own lifetime and now even several years after she's dead, have been consistently and universally slammed by the (same) reviewer *The Times* always seems to drag out for them! And slammed for the same reason that Jung's are: namely, she, and he, have had literally millions of enthusiastic readers, while the official books *The Times* wants you to buy—those awful English professor books about French theory or the latest inanity awarded the Booker Prize—barely even make it to the remainder pile.

So that's why I'm writing to you. I know that you have followed the subjects that Noll is writing about very closely, and I wonder if, as an advisor to this journal after all, you would be so kind as to tell us what you think of his book. We have a rule at *Spring* that we do not allow outsiders to submit book reviews (like most journals we are deluged with submissions from people who want to review their friends), so I am not asking for a review so much as an enlightened opinion. I think no matter what else we may think of Noll, he deserves at least that much.

Sincerely,

Sheila Grimaldi-Craig
Connecticut, Oct. 13, 1997

Dear Sheila Grimaldi-Craig,

Thank you for your letter requesting my views on Richard Noll's *The Aryan Christ*. Thank you also for not asking me to write a book review of it, so I don't have to decline this. I have given some thought to the subject, indeed, to the length of writing a book-length rebuttal (too many fallacies to get across in a review). Here is a description of it:

Sonu Shamdasani. *Cult Fictions: C. G. Jung and the Founding of Analytical Psychology*. London: Routledge, March 1998.

What is the Jungian movement? What relation, if any, does it bear to Jung and his original endeavour? It is sensationally alleged by Richard Noll in *The Jung Cult* and *The Aryan Christ* that Jung founded a cult based on his self-deification, which bears similarities to those around Jim Jones, Luc Jouret and David Koresch, and is alive and well in Jungian psychology today, which masquerades as a genuine professional discipline.

Cult Fictions presents the first accurate account of the founding of analytical psychology. Drawing on new documents, it follows the trail that led Jung to found the Psychological Club in Zürich in 1916. It recounts the controversies that ensued, and how Jung's followers reformulated his project. It assesses the evidence for the cultic allegations, which it demonstrates to be fallacious. It shows the relevance of this history to current concerns around the institutionalisation of psychotherapy, its societal legacy, and the widespread fascination with cults. *Cult Fictions* establishes a fresh agenda for the historical evaluation of Jung and his legacy.

You close your letter by stating that Noll deserves an enlightened opinion. I don't think it is Noll, but C. G. Jung who deserves this. From my perspective, the principal error of Noll's work is not that it is critical of Jung, but that it does not give a proper reconstruction of Jung's work on which to base an evaluation. It is just a cult fiction. If a man is to be hanged, surely he has the right to be judged on his own words? Common decency, let alone scholarship, would require that.

Best wishes,

Sonu Shamdasani
London, Nov., 1997

Stephen Karcher. *The Illustrated Encyclopedia of Divination*. London: Element Books, 1997. Pp. 256. Cloth, $25.

In what is without doubt the most exquisitely illustrated book ever done on this subject, Stephen Karcher has written a bold and intelligent study of the entire world of pre-scientific practices, from omens and symbols to shamans and seers, from reading the book of fates according to Tibetan dough-ball divination to acting out the subtleties of the Iriquois "religion of dreaming." No matter how much you may think you know about divination, nothing but nothing could prepare you for this book. Karcher, who has a Ph.D. in Comparative Literature from the University of Connecticut, brings a serious scholar's range to an area too often left to amateurs and dilettantes. His years of work with Rudolf Ritsema on the *I Ching* at the Eranos Foundation in Switzerland established his reputation as a cultivated and engaging writer, and their edition of the *I Ching* remains the most thorough and authoritative to date. But even readers of that work will be bowled over by the extravagant richness and endless surprises that come from turning the pages of this one: every detail of these bizarre customs and exotic rituals is so gorgeously illustrated, not only with a wealth of pictures but also with little side-boxes that explain how you might yourself—if you are game enough—do the same strange practice. (Our favorites: "Blowing Bad Luck Away," "Manjushri's Answer," "How to Divine With Dice," "Drumming Up," "Consulting the Ngam Spider," "The Cosmos of the Liver," and especially "Talking With Birds.")

"The first thing that happens is that the world comes to life. You enter a world of powers, potentialities, and presences in which your destiny and your actions matter. Things and events acquire the capacity to speak with you. The act and language of divination revive a lost world of soul, a world full of spirits, magical helpers, and significant landscapes. We acquire a sense of destiny, the means to negotiate with that destiny, and a guide or helping spirit in the process. The 'living world' begins to play an active role in our lives.

This mixture of fortune-telling, practical guidance, and spiritual advice may seem strange to us at first, with our culture's concern with great transcendental truths. It cuts across the usual boundaries between what is important and what is unimportant, for anything can become a place where the spirit world enters your life, and thus a matter for divining. The world you meet through divination is full of imaginative forces with attributes, powers, desires, and needs that are creating what we experience. Our souls ask us to recognize the events and emotions that sweep through our lives—as gifts of these forces, with lessons to teach and tolls to pay. Recognizing this, giving attention to these forces, is one of the great healing acts that divination has to offer us."

Jung on Active Imagination. Ed. by Joan Chodorow. Princeton: Princeton UP, 1997. Pp. 200. Paper, $14.95.

To their excellent "Encountering Jung" series of anthologies of Jung's writings on select themes (Jung on Evil, and Jung on Alchemy were published in 1995), Princeton has now added this invaluable collection. All the papers Jung wrote on Active Imagination" are included, from "The transcendent function" to his "Commentary on The Secret of the Golden Flower," from The Tavistock Lectures to excerpts from Mysterium Conunctionis. During his own psychological crisis following his break with Freud, Jung rediscovered play as the key to his unconscious. It is fair to say that all the art therapies the world practices today (painting, dance, poetry, and even sandbox) have stemmed from these writings. Jung writes:

"Every good idea and all creative work are the offspring of the imagination, and have their source in what one is pleased to call infantile fantasy. Not the artist alone, but every creative individual whatsoever owes all that is greatest in his life to fantasy. The dynamic principle of fantasy is play, a characteristic also of the child, and as such it appears inconsistent with the principle of serious work. But without this playing with fantasy no creative work has ever yet come to birth. The debt we owe to the play of imagination is incalculable." (Jung, 1921, par. 93)

Marie-Louise von Franz

1915 – 1998

New from Princeton

Painting by Christiana Morgan, from *Visions*

Visions
Notes of the Seminar Given in 1930–1934 by C. G. Jung
Edited by Claire Douglas

For C. G. Jung, the 28-year-old Christiana Morgan was an inspirational and confirming force whose path in self-analysis paralleled his own quest for self-knowledge. By teaching Morgan the trance-like technique of active imagination, Jung launched her on a pilgrimage of archetypal encounters in a quest for psychological integration—encounters she recorded in the words and brilliant paintings that formed the basis of the seminar Jung would give to his circle in Zurich.

Here the careful transcriptions of the seminar notes are combined with color reproductions of the visions paintings, offering an unprecedented view of Jung as a teacher and as a man. He speaks candidly in a dialogue with members of the seminar about the Morgan visions, even as he struggles with the feminine principle in his subject and in his own psyche.

"Here is Jung as he was giving everything he had (and that was such a great deal) to understand the psyche. And here is a noble editor worthy of him, Claire Douglas, to point out the inevitable limitations in even this great genius's ability to provide a lasting cultural hermeneutics of women's experience."—John E. Beebe, III, M.D.

Bollingen Series
41 color illustrations.10 halftones. 77 line illustrations.
Cloth $125.00 ISBN 0-691-09971-5
$95.00 prepublication price through December 31, 1997
Not available from Princeton in the Commonwealth except Canada

New in paperback
Translate this Darkness
The Life of Christiana Morgan, the Veiled Woman in Jung's Circle
Claire Douglas

Christiana Morgan was a muse who influenced twentieth-century psychology and inspired its male creators, including C. G. Jung, who saw in her the quintessential "anima woman." Here Claire Douglas offers the first biography of this remarkable woman.

Paper $16.95 ISBN 0-691-01735-2

Abridged paperback edition

Jung's Seminar on Nietzsche's *Zarathustra*

Edited and abridged by James L. Jarrett

With a new preface by William McGuire

The original two-volume edition of Jung's lively seminar on Nietzsche's *Zarathustra* has been an important source for specialists in depth psychology. This new abridged paperback edition allows interested readers to participate with Jung as he probes the underlying meaning of Nietzsche's great work.

"Nietzsche is perhaps the first Western man to have experienced a psychological encounter with the Self. . . . [This] seminar on Nietzsche's *Zarathustra* . . . [is a] magisterial enterprise [that] demonstrates to any perceptive reader Jung's millennial magnitude."—*Psychological Perspectives*

Bollingen Series
Paper $17.95 ISBN 0-691-01738-7 *Due January*
Not available from Princeton in the Commonwealth except Canada

Prometheus

Archetypal Image of Human Existence
Carl Kerényi

Translated from the German by Ralph Manheim

Prometheus the god stole fire from heaven and bestowed it on humans. In punishment, Zeus chained him to a rock, where an eagle clawed unceasingly at his liver, until Herakles freed him. For the Greeks, the myth of Prometheus's release reflected a primordial law of existence and the fate of humankind. Here Carl Kerényi examines the story of Prometheus and the very process of mythmaking as a reflection of the archetypal function.

This well-known book is now available in an attractive and affordable new paperback edition.

"A sterling example of classical scholarship, literary exegesis, and cultural inference. . . . Not only does this book tell us much about man, through his prototypical image, but also much about the Greek civilization which created Prometheus in its image."—*Contemporary Psychology*

Mythos: The Princeton/Bollingen Series in World Mythology
Paper$14.95 ISBN 0-691-01907-X *Due January*